THE WISDOM OF PELICANS

VIKING
COMPASS

Donald McCullough

THE WISDOM

A search for healing

at the water's edge

VIKING COMPASS

OF PELICANS

VIKING COMPASS
Published by the Penguin Group
Penguin Putnam Inc., 375 Hudson Street,
New York, New York 10014, U.S.A.
Penguin Books Ltd, 80 Strand, London WC2R 0RL, England
Penguin Books Australia Ltd, 250 Camberwell Road, Camberwell,
Victoria 3124, Australia
Penguin Books Canada Ltd, 10 Alcorn Avenue,
Toronto, Ontario, Canada M4V 3B2
Penguin Books (N.Z.) Ltd, Cnr Rosedale and Airborne Roads, Albany,
Auckland, New Zealand

Penguin Books Ltd, Registered Offices:
Harmondsworth, Middlesex, England

First published in 2002 by Viking Compass, a member of Penguin Putnam Inc.

10 9 8 7 6 5 4 3 2 1

Illustrations by Tom Leedy. Reproduced by arrangement with Tom Leedy.

CIP data available

ISBN 0-670-03103-8

Printed in the United States of America
Set in Esprit Book   Designed by Francesca Belanger

This book is printed on acid-free paper. ∞

To Shari

CONTENTS

ACKNOWLEDGMENTS

No book, not even the most personal, comes into being without a network of support. I'm thankful for those who have helped with this one: Kathryn Helmers not only contributed her considerable skills as a literary agent, but remained a loyal friend during my darkest days and somehow found the right balance between affirmation (to keep me writing) and criticism (to help me write better); Tom Leedy created the art that graces these pages and provided helpful comments on early drafts (my praise might be more effusive if he didn't so consistently beat me in tennis); and Carolyn Carlson and Lucia Watson of Viking Penguin provided important editorial assistance, as did freelance copyeditor Dave Cole.

In an indirect way, this book also owes much to a community who, during the hardest time of my life, walked alongside me and held me up and embodied the love of God: Woody and Stephne Garvin, Bob and Susan Long, Jim and Matilda McLaughlin, Tom and Martha Leedy, John and Diane Vinson, Scott and Becky Shaefer, Frank and Joan Drachman, Jim Stoltzfus and Floyd Humphreys, Dottie Black Schmidt, Sr. Maureen Brown, Arnold Come, Walter Johnson, Rachel Fitzgerald, Donald Burger, Bill and Carol Dew, Gary and Marily Demarest, Larry Grounds, Garry and Lynne Schmidt, Kay Kimball, Harvey White, Randy and Maria Zack, Ron White, Bob and Joanne Blackford, Bill and

Vivian Bell, Charlie Boss, Peggy Ngubo, Gayle Hall, Mary Elmore, and others, too numerous to list, who, with a telephone call or a note, offered timely encouragement and kept me from withdrawing into isolation. In the narrative that follows I have attempted to articulate complicated emotions; now that it's finished you would think I'd be practiced enough to express gratitude for these, my friends. But I cannot find words to bear the weight of my feelings, except to say, I love them.

I love my family, too. My parents, John and Ione McCullough, never wavered in life-giving nurture; my daughter and son-in law Jennifer and Geoff Ziegler have been generous in forgiveness, steady in encouragement, and have even produced my first grandchild, Timothy Geoffrey, a timely reminder of the miracle of new life; my daughter and son-in-law Joy McCullough-Carranza and Marino Carranza have worked through the pain of this season to reaffirm the bonds of our love. My sister and brother-in-law, Patti and Ken Blue, along with their eight children, have remained faithful. And my wife's children and their spouses—Julie and Gary Silverman, and Steve and Elyse Regan—along with her mother, Gloria Hall, and her sister and brother-in-law, Adrienne and Larry Hofreiter, have embraced me with affection and made me part of their family.

Finally, last on this list but first in importance, my wife, Shari: I cannot imagine surviving the turmoil chronicled in this book without her companionship. She is a true partner in my suffering and joy, and she has buried in my heart a great delight and constant thanksgiving and abiding love.

My heart in hiding
Stirred for a bird,—the achieve of, the mastery of the thing!

GERARD MANLEY HOPKINS

1

AT THE MARGINS

A brown pelican glides along the crest of a wave with unlikely grace. He is a large bird with an extravagant bill far out of proportion to the rest of his body. He seems misshapen, a victim of some evolutionary prank, an aerodynamic impossibility. Yet there he is, the tip of his wing caressing the edge of a wave, sailing with ease and dignity and even beauty.

More will likely follow, for they rarely fly alone. Another half dozen soon appear on the leading edge of the wave's curl. I watch, as I have for twenty years, and the more so now because I have nothing better to do.

Pelicans fly with regal bearing. They seem sure of themselves, confident of their place in the cosmos, unapologetic for their outlandish form. That form, on the other hand, turns the whole effect toward the comic, as though you had just come upon a king on his throne, attentive to the awesome duties of state, wearing the bulbous nose of a clown. You don't know whether to bow or laugh.

I choose laughter. God knows, I have had precious little of it lately.

It is my fifty-second year, and I have returned to the beach. I have always been drawn to the edges of land and water, the narrow strip between the two basic verities of earth. At an earlier time in my life, for fourteen years, I lived within walking distance of it, and during that time I ran thousands of miles along its shoreline, bodysurfed down hundreds of waves, and explored countless tide pools. The blue expanse and thunderous waves and squabbling gulls and pungent seaweed—these things and many more have always resurrected my senses, Lazarus-like, from the tomb of everyday routines.

Now, though, I seem drawn by something stronger than pleasure. A current is pulling me, inexorably, to this marginal place.

Recently, I have been entangled in a painful turn of events. Spectacular failures of mine and condemnation from others have, step by step, crushed much that I have known and loved, and like boots stomping through a bed of seashells have left behind only broken fragments. And my future is less certain than a sand castle at the water's edge. I have been forced into change I do not want, and though you might think this would make me long for stability, I seem attracted to a more abiding change, to a place where change is the norm, where it has been perfected through millions of years.

The beach is nothing if not change: tides advance and retreat, sometimes gaining ground, sometimes losing; shells and kelp are here today, gone tomorrow; gulls and terns and cormorants and snowy plovers and sandpipers come and go, as do bikini-clad sunbathers; breakers that gladden the hearts of surfers metamorphose into waves that delight body boarders and finally into distant relatives that lap at the ankles of infants. Rachel Carson said of life along the shore, "Only the most hardy and adaptable can survive in a region so mutable."[1] Perhaps this mutable world will provide clues for my own survival. I now need something more than a resurrection of my senses; I need to rise up out of a death in my being.

Most human actions spring from complex motives, conscious and unconscious; peel back one layer and another presents itself, often more influential than the one before it. My flight to the sea,

I realize, is also a flight *from* something. I am trying to get away, to find the farthest edge of my life. It would be more effective to board a freighter, but that doesn't seem to be an option. The next best thing is to go to the beach.

I am fleeing from what land represents because I am fleeing from myself. Six years ago I resigned as pastor of Solana Beach Presbyterian Church (near San Diego) to become president of San Francisco Theological Seminary. The professional transition was challenging, and the personal more so. A year after the move I confessed to my wife that I had dishonored our marriage vows. I admitted, with shame, that I had been unfaithful to her. In the ensuing months we tried to confront our problems, and we argued and cried and prayed and lost hope. There were days the sun never rose; darkness was all-encompassing. Finally, we separated and divorced.

My sorrow and guilt were pure, untainted by happiness. I continued to be affirmed for my work as a pastor, writer, conference speaker, and seminary president, and for the next couple of years I carried on with my responsibilities. From outward appearances, I suppose, I was still a success. But praise from others could not hush condemnation from myself. Alone at night, in a large, empty house, I had a large, empty hole in the center of my heart. I judged myself a complete failure.

Eventually, healing started to come. Therapists and friends surrounded me with wisdom and compassion and, unlike all the king's horses and all the king's men, were able to help put Humpty-Dumpty together again. I even sensed a divine smile of forgiveness directed toward me, and in this freedom I got up and started down a new road.

I did not get very far, however. News of my failure spread beyond a confidential few. It electrified the gossip wires, gathering force until formal allegations were lodged against me. These allegations provoked my denomination to form an "investigating committee," and by then it didn't matter that I had already repented and tried to make restitution and undergone therapy. Things began spinning out of control.

Which is exactly what they have been doing ever since.

That is why I am running from the land behind me. I am a middle-aged man without a job, without a self-identity, without a future, and without a clue about what to do with myself.

The pelicans seem to know what to do with themselves. They fly by, with feathers aglow in the afternoon sun and wings flapping only occasionally. The picture of peace.

I am not at peace. An emotional war wages within me. I'm grieved by the wrong I have done, and I'm angry at what has been done to me. My failure has caused great hurt and disappointment; some days my remorse is overwhelming. Nevertheless, condemnation from others has been so extreme, so beyond rationality and filled with hatred, that I find myself falling into defensiveness—and worse, damnable self-pity.

What do I expect? I caused a *sexual* scandal. Sex is more than a physical act. It is a force flowing through our subterranean depths, a river of dreams and fears and anxieties and fantasies and jealousies and longings that often floods the landscape of our lives. No one relates to it objectively, dispassionately. The word alone can alter breathing patterns, raise blood pressure, and cause an involuntary double take in the imagination. And the story of a *pastor* guilty of sexual misconduct can set off a volcanic explosion of molten emotion.

Still, I had hoped for more from the Church, the community that seeks to follow the teachings of Jesus and is officially committed to God's mercy and forgiveness and restoration. Where is this grace when *I* need it? Arms that intend to embrace can, with sufficient provocation, become weapons to deliver a roundhouse punch. Then again, the Church had hoped for more from me, too. I can hardly begrudge anyone the desire to knock me flat when I'm working so hard to knock myself flat.

And speaking of God, where is he (or she, as the case may be)? I feel abandoned and alone. The moment I say this, I hear a theological professor within me: "You are not alone, not really, for God is present with you even in this mess, and someday you will look back on this as a time of growth." I know this lecture by heart, have it frigging memorized, because I've delivered it many times to poor souls sitting on their own beaches. But soon the lecture is drowned out by something much louder: the silence. Where is God? *Who* is God?

I used to know much more about God than I do now.

What I know now are pelicans flying by, and sand cradling my butt and getting in my shoes, and the sound of waves breaking a few yards away. The confusion within me seems drawn to this place. A recent book on the beach describes it as "the infinitely creative junction of elements where habit and convention dissipate and imagination once again takes over. It is to the beach, in other words, that we go to reinvent ourselves."[2] Perhaps that's what I'm looking for: a place for my imagination to take over, a place where I can reinvent myself.

The vastness before me seems to promise expansive possibilities. I breathe deeply, hungrily drawing its atmosphere into every tiny twig of my lung's bronchial tree, trying to fill my whole being with its unknown potential. Human life emerged from this water, biologists say. Maybe renewed life can come from it now.

Looking toward the horizon, I am possessed of a conceit: with no obstruction in view, I behold so much, I seem to see far into the immensity. It is an illusion. In truth, the full sweep of my sight, from north to south and to the horizon, embraces only a tiny fraction of the ocean's surface. As for what lies beneath, I am blind; I observe no canyons or mountains, no plankton or shrimp or whales. At water's edge, waves of ignorance knock knowledge off its feet. The sea demands humility.

And respect. I have sailed upon it for many years, and though I love its beauty, I have learned to fear its dangers. It extends toward human life an indifference so absolute as to seem malevolent. It is unknown and unpredictable and unsafe.

So I echo E. B. White's question: "Why does the sea attract me in the way it does?"[3] I have no easy answer.

One word best describes the sea: mysterious.

This mystery, I think, is the fundamental attraction for me. It takes little imagination for it to symbolize a deeper mystery, the one behind or underneath or above the confusing events of my life, the unseen Mystery that holds and is at the center of all things.

Now I have reached the substratum of my motivation, the deepest reason my flight has taken me to the beach: I want—need, maybe—a physical manifestation of my spiritual situation, a kind of sacrament signifying the state of my soul. I am a man at the margins. I am standing on the narrow strand between my failure and my aspirations, between what was and what will be, between my previous certainties and my present confusions, between my humanity and the Mystery. I want to face this Mystery, to inquire of it, to wait until it might show the way into the future.

Anne Morrow Lindbergh says that by the water's edge "one becomes, in fact, like the element on which one lies, flattened by the sea; bare, open, empty as the beach, erased by today's tides of all yesterday's scribblings. . . . The sea does not reward those who are too anxious, too greedy, or too impatient. To dig for treasures shows not only impatience and greed but lack of faith. Patience, patience, patience, is what the sea teaches. Patience and faith. One should lie empty, open, choiceless as a beach—waiting for the gift from the sea."[4]

I will wait, then. I will be bare and empty, praying that today's tide will indeed erase yesterday's scribblings so I can begin to write the next chapter. I will even be patient, as patient as a hard-driving, achievement-oriented, success-calculating man can be.

I will wait for my gift from the sea.

Could it be these pelicans flying by?

I have always noticed them, but now I am noticing things in earnest, waiting for something I cannot describe, on a pilgrimage of sorts. My only vocation is to pay attention. So I watch as pelicans soar in untidy formation, sometimes three or four, sometimes thirty or forty. I watch as they fall from the sky, like dive-bombers, straight into the water. I watch as their pouches brim with water and writhe with fish. I watch as they launch themselves from rocks, always awkward and amateurish, until airborne and born again into creatures of elegance.

Pelicans have often been represented in stained glass and paintings and heraldry, presumably as an image of something more than themselves. Early Christians adopted them as a symbol of Christ's sacrifice on the cross, no doubt because of the legend that the mother pelican, if she cannot find food for her nesting young, will slash her chest to nourish them with her own blood. Are they now offering themselves for my nourishment?

I will learn more about these birds. Having moved back to San Diego, I am once again their neighbor. I will keep an eye on them, like a busybody with too much time on his hands, keeping track of all the comings and goings.

Pelicans, I discover, are survivors. They have been around a long while. Fossil remains indicate that *Pelecanus occidentalis* appeared about forty million years ago. That means they're about twenty times older than humans, our seniors by a considerable stretch of time. Among the first birds to evolve from reptilelike land animals, they survived a weeding-out process that has left only nine thousand species out of two million experiments. They have endured, wondrously so, notwithstanding the onslaughts of natural selection and even the deadly ways of humans.[5]

They have always been near water. They are not *of* water, like fish; they need land on which to mate and rear their young and congregate and rest. But they live *from* water, drawing from it all their sustenance. This dependency seems encoded deep within them; they will not stray from their source of life. At the end of the nineteenth century, A. W. Anthony, studying pelicans on the islands off Baja California, observed them at feeding grounds in a bay they could have reached by flying two miles over land but instead flew twenty miles to stay near water.[6]

Pelicans prefer the margins, it appears. They have survived, from before recorded history, at the narrow edge between land and sea. They testify to the possibility of survival, even renewal, in this in-between place.

I have always been a creature of the margins, I suppose. Now that my brokenness has overtaken me and I have lost much, I am simply more aware of what has always been my location. To be human, it seems to me, is always to feel oneself stranded between the familiar and the unknown, between failed opportunities and hoped-for possibilities, between regrets and longing, and most of all, between one's experience, bordered by sensory impressions and reasoning capacities, and the Mystery beyond.

Are pelicans telling me that I can find life at the margins? Are they able to impart the wisdom of healing?

I believe that's why they are here. Maybe I am simply projecting my own longings onto these birds. Or maybe the truth that is already within me is using them. Or maybe Mystery itself is speaking through them. Maybe it's not important to distinguish between these things. You can *maybe* anything and everything, when it gets down to it. There comes a time to set the *maybes* aside and plunge beneath the surface of things.

So I will keep watching and listening.

2

WILLIAM'S BILL

The bill, of course.

I must begin with this apparent defect, this aberration of nature. Sensitive readers may flinch. Isn't this like commenting on a stranger's birthmark? Dare I begin with something so . . . ahem, ugly?

I have no choice. It is impossible to ignore, being approximately the size of Rhode Island. You wonder if the Creator got around to it at the end of a very long day, after happy hour began and things got a little out of hand in the workshop. It is the bird's most prominent feature, the irreducible essence of pelicanhood. Cajun fishermen in Louisiana named him *grand gosier*—"big gullet"—and you don't have to look twice to see why. In the bird kingdom, this must be a source of embarrassment.

Imagine a young pelican—William, let's call him—wandering from the nest and falling in with squawking gulls. They hover around him, trying their pesky best to steal fish, until they realize he hasn't yet learned how to catch them. Their frustration turns to mockery: "Hey, freak-face, how'd you get a boat stuck in your mouth?" William is conscious of nothing but his mouth, the biggest mouth in the world and too heavy to hold up. He is all mouth, all mandible and pouch and throat; he is nothing but this . . . this mistake. He cannot lift his head for the weight of it.

But the pelican I now see flying across the surface of the water, holding an altitude of about one foot, has learned how to hold his head high, with bill lifted proudly in front of him like the nose of a Concorde. It's William, come of age. He's learned to fly with the monstrous thing. I'm impressed, and I ask him how he's done it. Hearing myself talking to him, I realize he's an "imaginary friend" for the little boy inside of me who, more than ever, feels alone on the playground.

I'm not alone, I know. Most people have something that seems an embarrassment, a source of shame. In the eighteen years I served as a pastor, hundreds of people sought my counsel, and I quickly learned that almost everyone carries a load of regret: over physical appearance, over past failures, over present circumstances, over painful relationships, or over a hopeless future. This feeling is so widespread I consider it part of the human condition, as prevalent as hunger or thirst.

We're caught in a paradox: to be fully human, to maximize ourselves, we must make choices, and yet the moment we do, we limit and narrow ourselves; to say *Yes* to one thing means necessarily to say *No* to other things. And then there are things other people choose, and things no one chooses but happen anyway. Thus we live in a tangled web of consequences, some of which we do not like, and we have a sense of incompleteness, and that incompleteness fills us with regret. Everyone has these feelings, as I say, but regret, in its most intense form, is always personal and fiercely private; it is over something *I* have done or something done to *me*. Regret isolates us, sets us apart from others. There is no bill quite so ugly, so embarrassing as mine.

Unless maybe it's William's. It may be hard to believe, but there is more to it than meets the eye. On the top is a hard mandible, about a foot in length, hooked at the tip, and underneath is a soft pouch for scooping fish out of water. This pouch is extremely flexible; it can distend to grotesque proportions, holding up to three gallons of water. In 1910 Dixon Lanier Merritt penned a now-famous limerick:

> A wonderful bird is the pelican,
> His bill will hold more than his belican.
> He can take in his beak
> Food enough for a week,
> But I'm damned if I see how the helican.

Overlooking Merritt's license with the facts (actually, the pelican doesn't store fish in his bill; after squeezing out the water, he swallows them for storage in his esophagus), it's easy to understand his amazement at the sight of a bird with a huge, bulbous pouch brimming with water and writhing with fish.

So William discovers, as he matures, that the bill that caused him shame, that once seemed so mistaken and misshapen, is really quite useful. It comes with a built-in fishing net. When underwater, he can open it and scoop in fish. What once embarrassed him to death now nourishes him to life.

Perhaps my imagination has carried me too far. I've undoubtedly projected my own embarrassment on this pelican flying by. I live with a mistake that seems out of proportion with the rest of my life, and the weight of it makes it hard to keep my head up. So I'm mesmerized by this pelican with an enormous bill, and this bill seems a symbol of an important principle: *the things that seem ugly, even painful, can become a source of life.*

I'm suddenly transported five hundred miles away, carried by memory to a small office in Berkeley. I'm sitting on a couch. Across from me is Rachel, my psychotherapist. She is a former

Roman Catholic nun, now a clinical psychologist and Jungian analyst. She is wearing a long, funky dress, with an odd necklace, and she radiates inner calm. For the last couple of years I've taken refuge in the sanctuary of this calm. I have poured out everything within me—a bouillabaisse of memories and dreams and emotions—and she has listened and understood, sometimes comforting and sometimes scolding, sometimes praying and sometimes cussing, and always she has been a rock to stand on as turbulent waters swirled around my neck, and I realize how much I have grown to love her. Psychologists would say it's transference, and no doubt they would be right. But she has mothered me, in a sense, helped birth me into new life, and my gratitude bonds me to her. She is repeating herself today, as would any good mother with something important to teach, singing again the cantus firmus of her psychotherapy, the message I know I need to learn: "Don, you have failed. Of course. You don't need me to tell you this. But now listen to me. Don't distance yourself from it. Don't run from it. The road to growth goes straight through it. Remember Dante. The only way to heaven is through hell. The way up is always the way down. Down, Don, all the way down, lower and lower, deeper and deeper into the darkness. It's not easy and it will hurt like hell. But I'm here to tell you it's the only way to heaven.

"You see, Don, you are *both* bad and good, shadow and light, sin and holiness, yin and yang—use any terms you want—and the way toward wholeness is not to run from either side, but to affirm them both, own them as part of yourself, and allow them to be incorporated into something larger."

My preferred method of dealing with ugliness has been to deny it. I have known it exists, theoretically speaking, and I can certainly spot it in other people. But I have not wanted to accept it as a possibility for *me.* I have seen myself as different, the exception to the rule. Failure is a reality, to be sure, but I have always had confidence in my ability to get over or around or through it; I have always, until now, seen my life on an upward trajectory, moving steadily toward the achievement of my dreams.

I'm a child of American culture. This is an officially optimistic society, one that worships at the altar of positive thinking. Anything—anything at all—is possible for those with a can-do spirit. In this land of opportunity go-getters *get* provided they have enough *go.* There may be difficulties, but those who stay in the race win the trophy. Believe in yourself. See yourself as good and beautiful and you will become good and beautiful. This theme is so familiar it bounces off our eardrums like Muzak in the supermarket—hardly noticed, simply part of the background.[1]

Educator and writer Parker Palmer has testified to the limits of this ideology: "I was raised in a subculture that insisted I could do anything I wanted to do, be anything I wanted to be, if I were willing to make the effort. . . . God made things that way, and all I had to do was to get with the program. My troubles began, of course, when I started to slam into my limitations, especially in the form of my failure." Parker then described how he was fired from a position as research assistant at the University of California, Berkeley. He was humiliated, but this embarrassment got his attention and forced him to face more of the truth about himself.[2]

Losing one's job in a humiliating way doesn't *necessarily* lead to an honest encounter with the truth about oneself. For me, the temptation to run from my darkness has been overwhelming. It's part of why I'm at the beach. St. Augustine said, "I had placed myself behind my own back, refusing to see myself,"[3] and if one of the towering intellects of Western civilization, a man with penetrating insight into the nature of God and the psychology of human beings, had to confess this, what chance do the rest of us have? We are skilled practitioners of the art of selective perception, repressing our fear and guilt and shame into the dark cellars of the unconscious.

Running from darkness does not mean running into light. The more we run from it, through denial or willful ignorance, the more its power grows. What Rachel was trying to tell me, and I'm slowly beginning to understand, is that we must enter the darkness, not be afraid to stay in it, and then—*only then*—will the light of knowledge have a chance to illuminate it.

The easiest way for me to escape my ugliness has been to focus on the ugliness of others. She is jealous. He is judgmental. She wants to distract from her own failures. He is a pompous ass who loves his little position of power. She is so blind to her own selfishness. His pride is worse than my adultery. On and on my thoughts go, punching and jabbing, and truth to tell, others have provided plenty of targets.

An inner voice tells me this will not lead to growth. *Consider William. He cannot deny his enormous bill. He cannot pretend it's as cute as a plover's or as trim as a sparrow's. It's always in front of him, an undeniable fact of his existence. All he can do is use it, allow it to become a means of drawing life from the sea.*

Personal renewal, the enlargement of our lives into greater wholeness, must embrace the entirety of our experience—our failures as well as our achievements, the good as well as the bad. This certainly cannot mean playing the silly game of pretending things are not so bad after all. ("Just think positive and everything will turn out great!") We need honesty, dedication to reality. Some things in life are just plain shitty, excuse my French, and all the euphemisms in the world will not hide the stench. By acknowledging the ugliness, by saying, "Yes, this, too, is part of my experience," we take the first step toward allowing it to become something more for us. Notice: I did not say something *different* but something *more;* negative things do not cease being negative, but they can be used for positive purposes.

Whenever I listen to the blues, I think of Ralph Ellison's description of this art form as "an impulse to keep the painful details and episodes of a brutal experience alive in one's aching consciousness, to finger its jagged grain, and to transcend it, not by consolation of philosophy but by squeezing from it a near-tragic, near-comic lyricism."[4] I cannot deny the jagged, sharp-edged grain of my life, but I want to finger it until it becomes something that catches the rhythm and tune of a new music.

A few months ago I decided, for obvious reasons, to reread Nathaniel Hawthorne's *The Scarlet Letter.* I remembered it as a fierce indictment of Puritan judgmentalism, and I was in a mood to do my own indicting. I did not get far into the novel, however, before I realized it's really about the quiet courage of an extraordinary woman.

Hawthorne begins the story as Hester Prynne, revealed as an adulterer by an untimely pregnancy, is led out of prison. "On the breast of her gown, in fine red cloth, surrounded with an elaborate embroidery and fantastic flourishes of gold thread, appeared the letter A."[5] She had been condemned to wear a scarlet letter, and so she used her skill with a needle to make it something impossible not to behold, a thing of beauty. She could not escape the fact of her failure; it would follow her the rest of her life. But she chose not to be a passive victim of condemnation. She claimed her failing, as it were, made it her own, drew it into the core of her being. And in the ensuing years, the letter, which set her apart from others, became a passport into the lives of others. People knew she had suffered, and they trusted her the more; she became a servant so skilled in her ministrations that some came to think the A stood for Able. Eventually, "the scarlet letter ceased to be a stigma which attracted the world's scorn and bitterness, and became a type of something to be sorrowed over, and looked upon with awe, yet with reverence too."[6]

Thomas Moore said that "Hester Prynne is the great sinner, publicly shamed by her community, but she embraces her fate, acknowledges her passion, and thus finds her life. Healing of the soul begins when men and women live their earthly reality instead of their ideas and ideals."[7]

My fingers are frozen in a grip around what I *wish* were true or believe *should* be true. It seems nearly impossible to pry them open to receive what *is* true.

For half a century I've been drawing a picture of myself and the world, and though I wouldn't call it a masterpiece, I do believe and trust it. Now I need to revise it. It may take more humility and courage than I possess. And yet . . . what choice do I have? I will need help from others, these pelicans and family members and friends and maybe even another Rachel. At some point, though, if I wish to claim my full potential, I will have to let go of ideals in order to be fully present to reality; I will have to awaken from dreams to face the day actually dawning. I will have to accept that I'm a pelican with an enormous bill, and then learn how to use the pouch that comes with it.

There are many things I wish were different. I wish I had not made foolish, selfish decisions in the past; I wish I had not hurt other people; I wish the Church had been more forgiving; I wish my reputation had not been torn to shreds; I wish my prospects for the future looked brighter. I wish I were not wearing a scarlet letter. I wish I did not have an ugly bill in front of my face. But I do. Any attempt to deny the reality of my circumstances, through selective perception or managing information or putting a favorable "spin" on events, will only prevent me from learning how to use the pouch connected with my failure.

My friend Frank Drachman has taught me the meaning of loyalty. His support has never wavered and never will. The earth will stop turning on its axis before he turns on me. I have always gone to him in my bleakest moments. The time has come for another lunch at our usual place—Jake's, on the beach in Del Mar.

While we wait for our orders I say, "Frank, this might seem an odd question, and I hope you won't think I'm insensitive, but has anything good happened to you because of your amputated leg?" Out of the corner of my eye I see beautiful, nearly naked bodies prancing in the surf and playing volleyball. I want to bite my tongue.

"Well," he says, "I need to tell you about Bill Veeck."

It was the spring of 1956. Frank had been discharged from the Army (after shrapnel from a North Korean bomb tore apart his leg) and Walter Reed Hospital, and was learning how to cope with a disability while starting law school at the University of Arizona. One day he received a telephone call from Bill Veeck, owner of the Cleveland Indians. Frank was surprised, to say the least. He knew Veeck was one of baseball's great ambassadors and the first to bring a club to Arizona for spring training, and he also knew that Veeck had lost a leg in a plane crash during World War II. Veeck said he wanted to meet Frank. Would he be willing to come to the Flamingo Motel? "And by the way," Veeck added, "bring your swimming trunks."

Frank thought Veeck probably wanted to see how his artificial leg worked, so he put on his trunks underneath his jeans and headed to the Flamingo. When Veeck opened the door to his room, he was dressed in nothing but his swimming trunks. His first words were, "Come on, Frank. Let's go swimming."

"I can't do that," Frank said.

"Why not?"

"Well . . . I mean, my leg and all, you know."

"Oh, don't worry about that. Follow me."

When they got to the pool, Veeck took off his artificial leg and jumped in the water. "Come on, Frank, it's great in here."

With a self-consciousness that made him sure the whole world was watching, Frank undressed and unfastened his artificial leg, and for the first time tried swimming with one leg. They swam and visited, talking about the challenges they faced.

Then Veeck said, "Frank, I've come to Tucson because I have something important to tell you. You can treat the loss of your leg as a tragedy or as the greatest asset in your life. If you decide to go forward unapologetic and unashamed, not letting it get you down, people will respect you. You will gain credibility. You will become an inspiration to others. Or you can allow this disability to be a tragedy, and that's exactly what it will be in your life. The choice is up to you."

Frank concludes by saying, "Bill Veeck changed my life. I decided to allow the loss of my leg to become something good. And that's what it has been—for forty-five years now."

Only God knows exactly how Frank's disability has influenced his life. What I can tell you is that he is a man of unusual strength, a man able to rise up, again and again, after severe personal losses—a devastating reversal in his professional work and the death of his daughter in a car accident, to name two—and to rise up with love and winsome faith.

·   ·   ·   ·

When I return to the beach, I see a pelican fly by and then circle back. I doubt it's William, but I suppose it could be. He rises to about thirty feet, stops in midair like a helicopter hovering, and suddenly plunges down into the water. He reappears with a pouch full of fish.

I remember Rachel's imploring me to go down into my pain, and Hester's ennobling of her scarlet letter, and Frank's walking with mercy into the lives of others. I think of ugly bills and how they can become dip nets into the Mystery, drawing up nourishment for survival and renewal.

And I breathe a prayer that I will have the humility to accept what is mine and the courage to dive deep into the sea.

3

DIVING DEEP

At the margins, it's easy to become passive. You're neither here nor there, and so you live in that "nowhereness" by being nonpartisan, uncommitted, aloof.

For many years I was the aggressive leader—inspiring others, making decisions, throwing myself into causes, spending my energy to help build institutions. Now let someone else do it. Some days, deciding which brand of deodorant to buy nearly paralyzes me. Whether from weariness or confusion, I'm content simply to sit by the water's edge. When at the beach, why not spread a towel and escape into sleep?

I launched one major offensive against this spirit of withdrawal: a year ago I was remarried. Marriage after divorce has been called the triumph of hope over experience. I made a commitment to Shari, to share my life with her, and thus I also made a commitment to the future, despite its uncertainty. I now look back on our marriage with some astonishment, somewhat like a sailor who set off on an around-the-world voyage and somewhere in the middle of the Pacific wondered where he ever found the courage to risk such an adventure. I'm grateful I found it at the appropriate time, or it found me, as the case may be, but now I feel depleted of it.

The day before yesterday I spent twenty minutes staring out the kitchen window, unable to decide whether to make myself a tuna or peanut butter sandwich, or whether to abandon the project altogether. Generals have committed troops to battle with less hesitation. I was paralyzed with indecision; opening a can or jar seemed to require more strength than I had. Writing a book, most days, is out of the question, beyond the realm of possibility, not unlike flapping my arms and flying. All I can manage is the next paragraph.

My grief has been a boulder puncturing my fuel tank, and now the engine is sputtering. Depression does that. An emotional cloud descends that has weight, a heaviness that makes doing anything difficult. I have no energy for the very things psychologists and self-help books recommend: I know I should eat balanced meals and keep exercising and cultivate a spiritual life and be faithful in my responsibilities. But I don't give a damn. It's easier to eat potato chips and watch TV. As for praying, God doesn't seem to be checking the answering machine; I'm not sure it's worth the effort to keep calling.

So it's off to the beach, once again. That will take all the energy I can find today.

I watch two pelicans appear just beyond a line of waves forming. Living in between is not the same as living inactively. These ancient creatures, who have survived at the margins for millions of years, are not passive in drawing life from the sea. They throw themselves into this work with such abandon it seems, to the observer, more like play. Let ducks paddle along the water's surface in search of food, and let gulls scavenge leftovers from other birds and fishermen. Wimps! Pelicans are of more elite company, like Navy SEALs or Army Rangers. They're the airborne divers of the bird world.

From twenty to forty feet above the water, or sometimes as

high as sixty feet, they plunge straight down, hurling themselves unreservedly, like suicide bombers. The descent begins with wings folded halfway back, feet held forward, and neck tucked back. As speed increases they elongate themselves; they flatten wings tightly back, pull feet under the tail, and stretch the neck forward. They turn themselves into aerodynamically efficient missiles rocketing toward the water. The tip of the bill points directly downward, and as it slices into the water it opens and the pouch expands and as many fish as possible are scooped in, along with two or three gallons of water.

Consider the variables: the bird must instantly calculate altitude and speed of descent, based on weight and desired depth of dive—*after* estimating the fish's size, depth, and speed through the optical distortions of water. Pelicans learn to do this only after much trial and error. Some never master the physics. Scientists think the failure of fledglings to learn how to fish is a major cause of brown pelican mortality, which seems to support reports of so many pelican bodies recovered not long after they have left the nest.[1] Given the complexities, it's amazing any of them do it.

And it's a wonder to behold. Not long after we were married, Shari and I were driving down the California coast. Near San Simeon we stopped to walk out on a pier that had been a favorite of hers for many years; she says it's a "thin space" where whatever separates the seen world from the unseen is unusually permeable, a place where spiritual realities can break in upon ordinary reality. So we were filled with expectancy, I suppose, but unprepared for what happened. Pelicans suddenly appeared—dozens of them, maybe hundreds, far more than we could count. They had spotted a large school of fish near the end of the pier, and the message had spread that there were more than enough for everyone. All around us, pelicans were dropping out of the sky, diving straight into the water, and coming up with fish. Some were solo divers and some flew in precision teams that plummeted in formation like Blue Angels. We were mesmerized, dumbstruck with wonder by the sight. As we walked to the car, Shari said, "See what I mean? You never know what's going to happen here."

Pelicans generally fly near the crest of a wave or at higher altitudes in formation with others. So when they are at a height of about twenty or thirty feet, in no discernible formation, moving slowly just outside the breaking of waves, I stop and watch carefully, almost hesitant to blink for fear of missing something. In an instant they upend themselves, pause slightly, as though sighting down their bills like a hunter down the barrel of a rifle, and then shoot themselves into the water, casting aside all caution, abandoning themselves to the depths. They manifest no moderation. They work within the disciplines of a craft, to be sure, but wholly unrestrained, with complete self-giving. They dive with passion.

Watching them, I have an inner disquiet I can't easily name. Could it be envy?

In this water's-edge season of my life, I feel cautious, tentative, as though I've just executed a first-class belly flop and am not sure I want to venture another dive. Smarting skin raises questions, urges hesitation. But for how long? Life, even at the margins, demands risk.

Diving pelicans suggest that renewal may be connected with a willingness to fling oneself wholeheartedly into the depths. There is an odd, paradoxical truth that those who find life are those who expend it. Throw yourself away and you somehow find more to give. Heaven seems to smile on those who lay down a month's salary on Blessed Dreamer in the sixth, or those who run each lap as though it were the last, or those who, against all logic, sacrifice themselves on the altar of lost causes. What Annie Dillard says about writing is true in general: "Spend it all, shoot it, play it, lose it, all, right away, every time. . . . Anything you do not give freely and abundantly becomes lost to you. You open your safe and find ashes."[2]

If we could break down the sap of life—the élan vital—into its various components, the way a chemist analyzes a compound, we would find it contains a large portion of pure, undiluted passion—a willingness to be used up and worn out for the sake of something. Life is conceived in passion, in more ways than one.

By "passion" I do not mean emotionalism. I'm thinking of something more profound and dangerous. The word comes from the Latin *passio* and the Greek *pascho*, which means suffering. The passionate give themselves so intensely toward something it hurts. In a way they lose themselves to that something, they die to it. It's as if they are carried outside themselves; in this sense they become eccentric.

Eugene Ormandy once directed the Philadelphia Philharmonic so vigorously he threw his arm out of joint. He plunged into the music the way a pelican plunges into the water.

The passionate care enough about something to stay with it. This is often what makes the difference between the mediocre and the excellent. Great artists demonstrate not only genius but tenacity, stubbornly following an idea into ever-deepening layers of meaning. Hearing the Beach Boys sing "Good Vibrations" is enjoyable (if this tune comes on the radio as I'm driving along the Pacific Coast Highway with my convertible's top down, I crank up the volume and the world becomes a mighty fine place), but imagine what a Mozart would do with the theme: he would state it in its simplicity, and then come back to it, again and again, from behind and from the side and from underneath, and just when it might seem he had exhausted all possibilities, he would surprise us with a whole new variation. He would stick with it, in other words, care enough about it to squeeze art from it.

But what if you lack this sort of commitment? What if you don't care enough to get up off the sand? What if you feel passionless? What if you feel too depressed, too emotionally tired, to throw yourself at anything?

I don't know. For now, I can only watch pelicans. They dive, and they keep diving. Sometimes they come up with fish, sometimes they don't. And maybe this, too: I can imagine what it would be like to be with them, rocketing myself toward the surface of the sea. Not toward the surface, exactly, but toward what's beneath, toward what's barely seen, toward the deeper mystery.

If I could rise to the necessary altitude and find the passion to dive, I would aim toward the mystery of myself and toward the Mystery of God. I doubt renewal at the margins can happen without plunging deeply into both of these bottomless realities.

Four years of psychotherapy have taught me a few things about myself—mostly, how little I know. In each person are deep currents, impulses and complexes and drives, and these give direction to the personality that floats on the surface. I have come to believe that the mysteries of being human coalesce around two primal feelings: fear and longing.

Woody Allen said, "The fundamental thing behind all motivation and all activity is the constant struggle against annihilation and against death. Death is absolutely stupefying in its terror and it renders any one accomplishment meaningless."[3] This fear may be the central building block in the foundation of our unconscious life. I recently came to this conclusion after reading Ernest Becker's *The Denial of Death,* a remarkable synthesis of post-Freudian psychoanalysis. In it he argues that "of all things that move man, one of the principal ones is his terror of death."[4] This fear is embedded deeply in the unconscious, beginning in infancy. The child is utterly dependent on parents. If needs are met, the infant must surely feel omnipotent, because all he or she has to do is scream and the discomfort is relieved by loving hands. But the child soon experiences frustrations to his will; he discovers he has no sure command over the actions of others; he thus feels weak, vulnerable, out of control. The cosmos then becomes overwhelming, even threatening. By about age three, the child has the capacity to be aware of death itself, though a favorable upbringing enables him or her to repress the terror.

Our "life project," Becker tells us, consists in somehow dealing with this reality. The way we do this is to "live on delegated powers," to transfer our hopes for defeating death to other persons, and even to objects and achievements. We all need to be "heroic," to be immortal, and so we look to parents or lovers or political leaders or pastors or celebrities—there are many options for stand-in heroes—to ensure our safety and help us "defeat" death.[5]

The reverse side of this fear is a longing for life. We have an insatiable hunger for more than we have, for something we cannot precisely define, for something just beyond our reach. This restlessness springs from the core of our being. It's as though there is a hole at the center, and its emptiness drives us toward things we hope will fill it. Another term for this is "eros." We long for completion, for fulfillment, for union with something or someone that will make us whole.

My depression is a kind of resignation to fear and retreat from longing. It's a willed mini-death, a laying down of arms in the war against annihilation and an exhausted retirement from eros. Renewal will only happen, I suspect, with a passionate plunge into the depths of my being; it will not happen—not, at any rate, with any permanence—without risky confrontation with my fear of death and a rekindling of my longing for life. Adultery was a terribly misguided flight from the one and attempt to find the other; romance and sex, for all their pleasures, did not satisfy these fundamental drives.

The greater and more important mystery is the one transcending all others, *the* Mystery: life-creating, vast, powerful, unpredictable, dangerous, beautiful, terrifying, largely unknown—the oceanic being we call "God."

The pelican launches herself in the sea, a laser-guided missile, straight into the depths of a darkness that nourishes. What, I must ask, gives her the courage? Is it instinct? Is it raw hunger? Is there simply no other choice for this creature? Has no one told her of the hazards of rocks and reefs and poisonous creatures and wayward fishing hooks? My questions are not idle; they spring from a confused heart, from the fear and longing at the bottom of my psyche. God has seemed more mysterious than ever, and standing on the shoreline I'm wondering whether I can follow the pelican in her plunge. Will my longing overcome my fear, and what will become of me if I dive?

I have always believed that God could not be contained within the cramped confines of my experience or understanding. As a college student I was drawn to the theology of John Calvin, in part because he had a big, sovereign God who inspired awe. As my study continued, I gravitated more to notions of transcendence than immanence, toward what Rudolf Otto called the *mysterium tremendum*. God, I soon learned, was vastly more than any human system could contain. When it came time to write a Ph.D. thesis at the University of Edinburgh, I explored the holiness— the absolute otherness—of God. And some years later I wrote a book about this, *The Trivialization of God: The Dangerous Illusion of a Manageable Deity.* No one needed to tell me that God was far larger and more complex than any human could fathom.

Still, I was a pastor and theologian, and as such I had developed firm convictions about the divine: though always mysterious, God has nevertheless provided a trustworthy self-revelation in Jesus Christ—a revelation that has manifested the loving and gracious character of God; God is like a father who cares for his children, even welcoming home rebellious prodigals, and like a mother, who with compassion and tenderness nurtures her young.

Then all hell broke loose around me, or if not *all* hell then at least part of it. I prayed, of course, asking for forgiveness and guidance, and every time I thought I understood where God was leading, I was wrong. Or at least unraveling circumstances made it seem thus. Perhaps God desired one thing and God's followers something else; perhaps God was indeed forgiving but God's people needed a pound of flesh out of my hide.

During a particularly discouraging week I was having lunch with a friend who had been through a similar situation. More white wine than I usually drink in the middle of the day loosened my tongue. "You know," I said, "I'm still attracted to Jesus—love him, even, and more than ever want to be his disciple—but I have to say, the followers of Jesus are a pain in the backside." He said he couldn't agree more, and that's why he had quit going to church. When he said good-bye that afternoon and hugged me hard and said, "Don, I love you," I didn't think to include him among the followers of Jesus; it didn't occur to me that that embrace in front of the restaurant was the closest thing to church either of us had experienced in a while. I had made a distinction between what God wanted for me and what people wanted to do to me; it was the only way I could keep my faith from falling apart altogether.

At three o'clock in the morning, however, this distinction isn't easy to maintain. A question troubles me, takes me by the throat and won't let go: Where is God in all this? If God is sovereign, why hasn't the divine arm reached down to direct my situation? Why didn't God protect me from my own vulnerabilities, and why hasn't God prevented this mess that seems to be growing like an out-of-control oil spill? I have always trusted that God was on my side, but now I have enough evidence to question this. I don't doubt that God loves me in the most general sense, as in "God so loved the world," but I am finding it hard to believe the part about every hair on my head being numbered. Why has God abandoned me?

My real problem isn't with a Church bureaucracy that has drifted far from anything resembling pastoral compassion; my real problem isn't with the entanglement of personal and political agendas with the central issues of repentance and redemption. *My real problem is with God.* That's what energizes my anger toward God's representatives, I must admit. After years of serving God, why hasn't God shown up to lend more support? It wouldn't have taken all that big a miracle to ensure a better outcome. The prayer of St. Theresa, after she had been thrown off her horse into a creek, keeps going through my mind: "Lord, if this is how you treat your servants, it's no wonder you have so few of them." Most of all, I hear the words of Jesus on the cross: "My God, my God, why have you forsaken me?" Didn't he undergo that abandonment for me, in my place, so I wouldn't have to? That's what I have preached and taught and wrote. Was I mistaken? Where is God? *Who* is God? I hope Tennyson was right in saying, "There lives more faith in honest doubt / Believe me, than in half the creeds."[6]

Not long ago I read a book by Alan Jones, dean of Grace Cathedral in San Francisco, and in it was a sentence that ambushed me: "What we need is a radical sense of exile—separation, distance—if we are to be saved from the illusion that we are at the center of reality."[7] Has all my questioning come from a childish illusion that everything should revolve around me? Is the Mystery up to something big, *really* big, and mercifully teaching me that I'm only a small, expendable part of it?

Personal misery, whether small or large, always distorts perspective; no problem ever seems as large as your own. Hammer your finger instead of the nail and no pain in the world will have a firmer grip on your attention. My thumb is bruised, that's all; my distress is nothing but a tiny grain of sand on an immense beach of suffering. But this only leads to deeper, more difficult questions about God. If God hasn't spared other poor souls, why bother with me?

By the water's edge, I look across a very large ocean: some days its expanse whispers possibilities and hope rises within me. Other days, though, I'm aware of how deep is the sea and how little I see, and in the center of me is a quiet trembling.

4

TAKING OFF

I have learned to spot pelicans in flight from a great distance, when they are scarcely more than specks in the sky. This is because of their singular grace. They glide along with fluid beauty, wings touching the sky as a ballerina's toes brush the floor—unlabored, lissome. Fred Astaire in the air.

Getting up there, however, is another matter. Gravity seems the pelicans' only natural enemy, and this foe launches its fiercest assault when they try to rise from its clutches. Although the brown pelican is the smallest of seven species worldwide, with a wingspan of six and a half to seven and a half feet, it is still a large bird. When those wings stretch for takeoff, you want to duck. You also want to avert your eyes, as an act of courtesy. What follows will be a mess.

I asked my friend John, who was a naval flight instructor, if there is a term for pilots who botch takeoffs, other than "dead."

"Yes," he said, "engineer or salesman—anything but pilot."

When a pelican beats the air with his wings, violently flapping with hysterical energy, desperately doing whatever necessary to get airborne, you wouldn't think of an engineer, a position implying far too much precision. You might think of a salesman, perhaps, but only a nervous creature ringing his first bell at the beginning of a door-to-door career; you're torn between compassion and disgust, and pretty sure it will end in heartache. A pelican trying to get off the ground is an ornithological embarrassment.

There is a large rock where pelicans congregate near La Jolla Cove. It's a great place to watch them, but the ceaseless coming and going causes me anxiety. Every takeoff causes a catch of breath and skip in heartbeat; I'm tempted to close my eyes, the way Shari does during violent scenes in movies. I gain a sudden sympathy for air-traffic controllers at O'Hare or Heathrow.

Why do they attempt it? The young ones, I mean, the birds that have never before risen in flight?

When William is about twelve weeks old, Mama and Daddy stop bringing fish to the nest. He doesn't have to be the brightest chick in the colony to know it's time to leave home. So he decides to get adopted by more caring parents, and he struts into a nearby nest as though he had a right to be there. No one is much interested in him. All eyes are focused on the writhing bulge in Neighbor Mama's pouch. With a couple of well-placed wing punches he fights his way through a noisy trio of youngsters, and without even a "Good morning, nice to see you, ma'am" thrusts his head deep into her pouch.

Scooping a meal out of a stranger's mouth is more difficult than you might imagine. For one thing, it's darker than a moonless night, and for another, you never know what you're going to find. Slick green stuff, maybe, or thistly critters.

William lunges for the biggest moving thing he finds and snaps his bill around it. What he catches is the bill of another pelican who has dipped in from the other side. Which creates a big problem. He's not sure what to do, so he holds on until he thinks of a plan. Neighbor Mama has one of her own, and with a quick jerk of her head sends him rolling in the opposite direction. Before he can get up, a wing comes down on his head and a bill wallops his backside.

He decides it's time to go back home. Before reaching the nest, he sees Mama standing alone on the sandstone with her head buried under a wing. She is preening herself, using the hooked tip of her bill to apply oil from her glands to her feathers. She lifts her head. He is close enough to see the rim of pink flesh around her eyes. He keeps walking toward her, acting as famished and near death as he can, begging for help by his pathetic appearance.

What she does is this: she turns away from him, spreads her wings, and with four or five harsh flaps flies out of his life.

William stands motionless as a rock. Minutes pass, maybe hours. He has no idea where to go, so it seems best to go nowhere, not even to move, until something moves with him. Eventually something does, and like a wave gathering height and force, it becomes a resolution that will not be stopped until it spends itself on an unknown shore. It is time to go to the water. He is a pelican, and pelicans find food in water. He will get his own food, yes, he will, and he will use his own pouch to pull fish from the sea, yes, he will, and he will begin his career as a fisherman. That's what he will do.

There is only one slight problem: he has no idea how to get there. He is standing on the ledge of a rock cliff that drops straight down. He wants to walk to the water; he wants a safe trail leading to a pleasant beach. But this is something you don't find in a rookery. They expect you to fly—a fine theory, no doubt, though unimpressive if all you've ever done is flap your wings when goofing off.

Where does he find the courage to do it? What drives him to attempt the impossible, to stretch wings and beat air and push feet and twist body—all in a mad effort to rise skyward? Is it instinct honed through forty million years of natural selection? Or is it desperate, gnawing hunger? What drives William and his friends to keep trying, despite clumsy awkwardness and crash landings and the risk of death?

What drives me? The instinct is human, too, make no mistake about it. The drive to rise higher and higher, the hunger. Hunger for what? It's not easy to say. "You don't know quite what it is you do want," Mark Twain wrote, "but it just fairly makes your heart ache you want it so." Who has not felt this so acutely that the inner emptiness assumes a shape and weight that is not *nothing* but *something*, something that torments and troubles one into perpetual restlessness? As Bertrand Russell expressed it, "The center of me is always and eternally a terrible pain—a curious, wild pain—a searching for something beyond what the world contains, something transfigured and infinite, the beatific vision—God. I do not find it, I do not think it is to be found, but the love of it is my life; it's like passionate love for a ghost. At times it fills me with rage, at times with wild despair; it is the source of gentleness and cruelty and work; it fills every passion I have. It is the actual spring of life in me."

Some would call this the glory and burden of being human, the inheritance of an evolutionary drive toward higher levels of being. Some would call it the lingering trauma of being taken from Mother's breast. Some would call it the consequence of alienation, the sign of separation from our true selves or from God. Some would call it punishment for eating the forbidden fruit and getting thrown out of the Garden of Eden. Some would call it homesickness for heaven. Some would call it proof of our need for union with the great All. Call it whatever you want. If you listen to your own heart, you won't deny its reality.

Restlessness may be expected in the valley of disappointment. The great shock of my middle years has been to experience it on summits of achievement. After preaching a stirring sermon. After making love with passion. After spending a day with my children. After celebrating Christmas. After hearing Bach's *Mass in B Minor*. After sailing on a clear day with twenty-knot winds. After holding a newly published book in my hands. After laughing with a friend. After all the best things, *especially* after the best things, a longing remains, stubborn and merciless.

This is my dirty little secret. I always want more.

This persistent desire is not generally a rude guest at the party, just a quiet one whose sullenness casts an unmistakable gloom over the whole affair. Carl Jung said this emptiness is the central neurosis of our time; that I'm not alone, however, is scant comfort.

I'm trying to stare down this impulse until it either retreats or explains itself. I suspect it's a manifestation of a love the Greeks called eros. Christians grant eros little respect; their tradition generally tosses it aside as an inferior love, selfish and self-seeking, as contrasted with agape, the love flowing eternally from God that is other-directed and self-sacrificing. I do not dispute this ranking. It's time, though, to pick up eros, dust it off, and restore it to its rightful place. This will not be easy, especially today, when it lives in troublesome proximity to another word—erotic—that immediately brings to mind sex or pornography.

Originally, eros referred to a fundamental drive in human nature. In Greek mythology Eros was one of the oldest gods, the creator of life on earth, born from Chaos but personifying harmony. Eros symbolizes the force within us that strives toward life and wholeness. In the words of Rollo May, "Eros is the drive toward union with what we belong to—union with our own possibilities, union with significant other persons in our world in relation to whom we discover our own self-fulfillment. . . . Eros is the longing to establish . . . full relationship."[1] It is a source of both pleasure and misery—pleasure because it finds enough satisfaction along the way to renew hope within us, and misery because too often it leads down painful, dead-end roads.

Eros is so thoroughly associated with romantic love in general, and sex in particular, because this is where it expresses itself most intensely. The longing of a man to move from estrangement to reunion finds something close to fulfillment—as close as he is likely to find this side of heaven—in the actual penetration of another person. The hunger of a woman to transcend fragmentation in a higher wholeness finds something close to fulfillment in the "filling up" she receives from her lover.

That this experience is only *close* to fulfillment by no means diminishes its significance. It may not be readmission to the Garden of Eden, but it's holding a rose and being mesmerized with delight by deepening layers of color and otherworldly fragrance. It may not be the banquet table of the Kingdom of God, but it's eating caviar and drinking excellent Bordeaux. This may be something of what St. Paul was getting at when he wrote of the spiritual significance of marriage, saying, "The two shall become one flesh. This is a great mystery, and I am applying it to Christ and the church."[2] Sexual union takes part, in some unfathomable way, in the union between the divine and the human.

So eros naturally becomes erotic; as a magnet points toward true north, the longing within us turns toward the sexual, to the happy conjunction of biological and spiritual drives, to the place where it is likely to find at least temporary satisfaction. But to understand what's *really* happening in the erotic impulse, we must see the direction of its trajectory. It's not really heading downward toward bed but upward toward something higher. "The movement of eros is always upward," Frederick Buechner has written. "Eros is the love of what is beautiful, the love of what is true, the love of what is good, the love of what is missing and necessary. . . . Eros is ultimately the upward-reaching, inexhaustibly yearning love of a man for what is infinitely desirable, and in that sense for God."[3]

To relocate eros from Times Square to heaven may be too much the work of self-justification. Perhaps my ability to philosophize, along with too much time on my hands, have come up with this theory to ease my guilt. I have enough self-doubt these days to question everything, especially my own ideas and motives. Am I only trying to explain away the lustful depravity of my life?

I don't think so. The restlessness within me, as deep and insistent as William's impulse to fly, has been a manifestation of eros. However immoral its expression, this eros has really been a desire for the highest, for God.

This doesn't absolve me. I'm still responsible for following the impulse down a dark, dangerous alley that could lead only into a cul-de-sac of suffering. To understand its cause does not make it excusable. I should have known it would be a botched takeoff that would never really get me airborne.

Frederick Buechner continues his description of eros by saying that if he were asked to produce a picture of it, he would choose "a little engraving by William Blake which shows the tiny figure of a man standing on the great, curved flank of the earth's surface. It is night-time, and the man, with his arms outstretched, has his foot on the first rung of a ladder which reaches up toward the moon. Underneath, in block capitals, are the words: I WANT! I WANT!"[4]

I am that little man. I see myself in his discontent and in his stretching toward the unreachable. I have wanted to rise higher, to get off the ground, to fly.

Now that little man is near death. Depression has suppressed much of my desire. Grief over failure and loss makes me cower before risk. After a crash landing or two, a bird is wary. Better not to attempt it; better to stay on the ground and be safe, to quash, or at least radically modify, all dreaming and hoping and striving. But without risk eros suffocates and dies, and without eros there is even less willingness to risk. Depression stirs a downward spiral. Perhaps this is not as bad as it sounds, because with no drive for life, there will be no disappointment and pain. It is peaceful in the grave.

I see the pelican's wild flailing at the wind, a comical or perhaps tragic attempt at the impossible. But he will not let passion die in the despair of failed attempts. He turns into the wind and shapes his wings just so, cupping them to climb the currents, and pulls back his neck and pushes with his feet. He tries this and that, discovering the disciplines of flight, and then—surprise!—he's off the ground, and he mounts the wind to achieve union with something more than himself, a fulfillment that, however short-lived and partial, enables him to become . . . a pelican, a *pelican,* for God's sake!

My restlessness, my longing, my hunger for more, my striving to rise skyward, my standing on the flank of the earth with arms outstretched toward heaven—these things must not be buried, not by grief or guilt, not by fear or fatigue, not by anything. I cannot allow eros to die. Only by flying higher will I be able to dive deeper into the Mystery that alone can satisfy my hunger.

The danger lies not in wanting more but in wanting the wrong things.

Running along Torrey Pines Beach, I spot a gull flying by. With a spastic contortion of his body, he twists and jerks and seems barely able to stay aloft. A fish is in his bill, head hanging out one side and tail flailing out the other. It is a big catch, maybe the biggest of his life, and now he not only has a large meal but a large dilemma. He flies toward the beach and starts to descend, knowing he can't hold the squirming meal much longer. Then he realizes that if he lets go he'll never get hold of it again, and so he heads back out across the water, as though still in control of the situation, as though a plan might be found farther up the beach. Once again he flies back in to the beach, and then out again. Back and forth, back and forth. I feel sorry for him, I really do. I know what it's like to cling to something I can't carry but am afraid to drop.

He caught the wrong fish, that's all. That's no reason to kill the hunger. The hunger is what gets the bird out of the nest and onto the ledge, what emboldens him to beat the air and rise and maybe someday learn to catch the right meal, what keeps him struggling to become an authentic creature of flight.

William steps cautiously toward the edge of the cliff to survey the situation. Below, the green sea gathers in darkening swells and crashes against rocks worn so deeply they are out of view. He has never seen anything so terrifying, and he thinks he isn't *that* hungry, when a gust of wind catches the bottom of his pouch and jerks his head so hard his feet slip out from under him. Suddenly he is tumbling through air. From sheer instinct he extends his wings, like a proper pelican, but pulling out of a free fall is not the easiest maneuver, especially if it's the first you've tried. His wings only straighten his descent and increase his speed.

Later he will learn you're supposed to break the water with the tip of your bill, so your pouch and head and body can slide wedgelike into the water. What he does now is duck. As he pulls his head down, his bill moves too far behind him, and instead of entering the water, he slides across the surface of it, causing his body to flip over and smash in a perfect back flop.

He is too stunned to move. A wave lifts him and heaves him against a hard, slimy rock. The first blow rolls him over. The second provides the inspiration he needs to start kicking his feet as fast as he can. If he doesn't get away from the rocks and waves, he will be pounded to pieces. It doesn't occur to him that he is actually swimming until he has gone far enough to rest. "I'm not sinking," he tells himself. "I'm on top of the water and not going down, and I can get around by moving my feet."

He floats into a quietude, a kind of reverie. He remembers his fall, and the chill that pierces him isn't from water. But there is something deep inside him that won't let go of it, a primitive instinct, a hunger for something more than fish. He imagines what it must be like to stay aloft, to soar with other birds, to rise high above the sea. And he knows he will try it again. Maybe tomorrow. He will find the correct angle for his wings, the precise rhythm of the flapping, the way to use the wind to lift him. He will become a pelican.

5

RITUALS

OF PREPARATION

The pelican twists her neck and rubs her bill on her back. What is she doing? I notice she does this constantly, like an odd tic, and I wonder about it. When I consult my books, I discover she is "preening." She has oil glands, and with her bill she is lubricating herself. Several times a day she runs her feathers through her mandibles, "somewhat like a zipper," in the words of one ornithologist.[1] Why does she do this? Is it adolescent vanity, akin to a teenager's ministrations of mousse and comb in solemn devotion to Perfect Hair?

No one is certain. Perhaps it creates healthy plumage. Perhaps it provides waterproofing and insulation. Perhaps it *is* cosmetic, primping for purposes of attracting a mate. Whatever the reason, preening is a ritual of preparation. Pelicans oil feathers to get ready for something, whether cold water or a hot romp. They rub the bill on preening glands and transfer oil to each feather; they brush head-feathers, which cannot be reached with the bill, directly onto the glands. There is a method, a daily discipline.

I remember quoting Winston Churchill in a sermon years ago: "Success is never final; failure is never fatal; it is the courage to continue that counts." That sounded true enough at the time;

now I'm not sure. Failure, it seems, *can* be fatal. But if Churchill was correct, what constitutes *continuing* for me?

For now, it probably has to do with getting ready, oiling my feathers for some future purpose. "God," said Martin Luther, "can shoot with the warped bow and ride the lame horse." Even use, presumably, a broken depressed sinner the Church has rejected. God never seems as finicky in these matters as some of God's followers; if the Bible can be believed, God doesn't mind using unsavory characters for noble ends.

In late winter William feels an inner urge, a hunger for something more than fish. He notices a pelican on the far side of the colony, festooned in bright colors. The bird is different, wonderfully different, *interestingly* different. And he wants her. So he moves toward her, following an ancient script inscribed on his genes.

He stands before her and follows a ritual as solemnly and carefully as a novice priest. He displays his pouch in all its variations, extending and contracting it, and he stretches his wings and draws them in. And he moves his head up and down and back and forth, tracing a figure eight, the symbol of infinity, which is nearly as far back as the routine goes. His father did it this way, and his grandfather, and his great-grandfather, back generation after generation for forty million years. Who is William to challenge tradition?

She will not accept his advances, not at first; she is no cheap date, no loose bird. She has standards, too, and is following her own script. She will demand of him ten or twelve tries before accepting his proposal and the nesting site he has chosen. When she does, they enter into an engagement of sorts, a mutual understanding of more grave and gratifying things to follow.

The next, often time-consuming stage of the courtship has no time for slow dancing as the sun sets over the ocean. They tend to more serious business with a dance of aggression, a theatrical performance demonstrating the willingness of each to protect the nest and drive away intruders. William has to be careful here. If he's too earnest, he will frighten her away. Who wants to live with a violent brute? On the other hand, if he's too gentle, too overly submissive, too much the "caring, sensitive male," his competitors will consider it a sign of weakness and invade his territory to seduce her out from under him.

There is ritual in this, as I say, a liturgy to follow. Hormonal instincts may rage, and for all I know, copulative urgencies may be wildly insistent. But William keeps it all under control. After the head-swaying and aggressive dancing comes the ceremony of the twig. He drops a single one in front of his bride-to-be. If she accepts, wedding bells chime and nest-building begins in earnest. Then William brings more twigs, some small and some large, and she starts constructing their home. Occasionally, he might try to insert a twig in the wall of the nest to show his own artistic abilities. It will come as no surprise to male readers that she accepts his gesture with courtesy, perhaps a condescending smile, and then when he's headed back out for another twig rearranges it to her liking.

During the construction of the nest, it's not all work and no play. Comes a day when William has had enough of twigs and wants a connubial romp. So he bows, ever the gentleman, and if she is agreeable she returns a curtsy. Then foreplay begins with rowdy enthusiasm. It gets rough, the equivalent of leather and whips. As William mounts her, he grabs her neck with his bill, which she apparently finds a major turn-on, so she moves her tail feathers to one side, as though slipping off her panties, to allow access. Five to fifteen seconds later, it's over. Bad news for the missus, I suppose. However, I feel obliged to mention, in William's defense and with some awe, that they can do it four or five times a day. To the casual voyeur, it might seem intemperate, even riotous. But the careful observer discovers that pelicans mate like proper Presbyterians, decently and in order—according to rules, following canons of convention.

It's all for the future. Courtship, mating, building and tending the nest, laying eggs—in all this males and females work together, following long-established routines, in anticipation of new life.

Pelicans make these preparations out of instinct, out of an entirely natural, unthinking behavior. I envy this. I'm not as holistic; I'm terribly divided between mind and emotions. My brain tells me things are not as bleak as they seem. I was, after all, a pastor for many years, and I witnessed firsthand the surprising capacity for human survival and renewal. But when my gizzard takes over, I expect the new day dawning will be dark and stormy, and the only way to face it will be to pull the covers over my head and pretend it's not happening. So I bounce back and forth. One day I determine to get a grip, and I tell myself something good is coming, and if I adopt disciplines that orient my life toward the future, I might at least create conditions that make renewal more probable. And the next day I say, "What the hell."

Contending against this dichotomy is probably useless. I am depressed, and giving myself the "Cheer up!" pep talk will be as effective as the Polish Cavalry against Nazi Panzers. I have lost much, and loss leads naturally to grief, and grief leads naturally to depression. There is a sense in which emotions just *are*: they're present whether you want them or not, unbidden, with an annoying will of their own. They may be like Jessie, my stepdaughter's dog. Last Sunday she approached me with a Frisbee in her mouth, inviting me to play catch. I tried to pull it out of her teeth, but she wouldn't let go. The harder I tugged and yanked, the tighter she held. I told her she was a stupid dog, that I couldn't throw the Frisbee if she wouldn't let go, and the more I struggled for control, the more fiercely she gripped it. Then I gave up and walked away, and she dropped it immediately. Perhaps that's what happens with certain emotions. Grasp depression in a fierce determination to yank it out of your life, and there will be something that sinks its teeth ever more deeply into it. But perhaps—I'm not sure of this, it's my hope—if you lose interest in the fight, walk away to focus on something else, the jaws that hold it will relax.

So maybe what I need to do is give up the fight. Let depression have its way and in the meantime focus on something else. Walk away from it. There may be things I can do now, regardless of my emotional state, that will orient me toward the future; there may be twigs I should be gathering for a nest in which new life will hatch.

I would rather wait until I'm in a better mood. I'm inclined to sit here at the beach, doing very little, and wait for some inspiration to strike me, some new enthusiasm that will get me up and moving. But I suspect that's not how it works. Rollo May, in a study on creativity, says inspiration, that sudden flaring of the unconscious toward new images and ideas that often occurs in moments of relaxation, almost always comes to those who have been struggling, who have been sitting at desks or standing at easels or working the clay.[2] If Einstein's greatest ideas came while he was shaving, as he confessed to a friend, it was because he had put in plenty of time with his books and calculations. In-spiration follows disciplined labor, in other words. Self-imposed limitations are necessary for freedom. Igor Stravinsky, referring to his experience composing music, said, "My freedom will be so much the greater and more meaningful the more narrowly I limit my field of actions and the more I surround myself with obstacles. Whatever diminishes constraint diminishes strength."[3]

Sailing on San Francisco Bay a few years ago, I had an unfortunate encounter with an out-of-control boom. The wind suddenly shifted and caught the back side of the mainsail, sending it flying across my boat. Naturally, I reached up to slow it down. Stupid move. Certain laws of physics went into effect—laws that, however necessary and wonderful in holding the universe together, proved troublesome in this particular instant. My upper arm snapped.

With my arm in a brace as a result, I couldn't lift it, and consequently, when the brace was removed a few months later, I still couldn't lift it. My shoulder had frozen. Twice a week I had to visit a physical therapist, a cute, sweet-spirited young woman who treated me as gently as a linebacker sacking a quarterback. She pushed, pulled, and punched with torturous efficiency. "Are you doing your daily exercises?" she always asked. "Yes," I would say, which was mostly true. I had a rope-and-pulley contraption set up in my bedroom, and I was supposed to pull down with my left arm in order to raise the right. I forced myself to do this day after day, forced myself into pain in the hope that my shoulder would again become flexible. There were many weeks when I lost faith and decided it was useless; I was sure it would never get any better. For some reason, though, I kept up the regimen, until one day I noticed I had reached for a can of shaving cream on the top shelf—with my right arm.

Okay. Perhaps I need to exercise today on behalf of a possible healing tomorrow. Wayne Gretzky, the legendary hockey player, said, "I always skate to where the puck is going rather than to where it's been." I want to do this, presuming the puck is actually going somewhere, presuming the Mystery behind and in all things is really aiming for the goal. But what should I be doing? Are there routines I should be following as regularly as a pelican oils feathers?

Three things come to mind. I'm not sure these are the most important disciplines for me, but nowadays, if I wait for certainty before acting, I'd never get out of bed in the morning. For all I know, these patterns of behavior are simply holdovers from my earlier life and ways for guilt to continue its harassment. I have nothing else to go on, however, than my intuitive feelings and rational thoughts, and though these may be as screwed up as the rest of my life, they are what I have to work with. And it's possible the Mystery might be in these, too.

The first is obvious. I should attend to my body. Everyone knows there is an intimate connection between the physical and emotional realms. In countless pastoral conversations I've encouraged depressed persons to eat well-balanced meals, get plenty of sleep, and most especially, stay on a program of exercise. I've often told about a man who was so depressed he decided to commit suicide by running himself to death. He went out and ran as hard as he could, and of course, he only passed out. So he went out again the next day, and the day after that, always with the same result. But instead of finding a more effective means of self-annihilation, he started to feel better. So he kept up his routine until he ran himself into mental health. I'm not certain this story is true, though I've heard it and told it so many times, I hope it is. In any event, it underscores the truth that exercise helps the emotional condition. There is a biological reason for this: aerobic conditioning releases endorphins, the brain's natural morphinelike hormones that heighten one's sense of well-being.

I have run for twenty-six years. Lately, though, I have been tempted to quit. My feet have started hurting and my knees and hips have felt stiff, and there are too many days I'm actually feeling my age. With all that has happened in the past few years, I'm just plain tired. Worn out, pooped. Some days, putting on running shoes requires too much effort, not to mention enduring the first few miles as my muscles and joints argue. But I'm determined not to surrender. Perhaps this is an obsessive-compulsive abnormality, or perhaps this is an important discipline of preparation. Whatever, I will do my best to keep running. I can do it at the beach, after all, and keep my eyes open for pelicans. And if my feet give out, I will try walking.

I'm also feeling called to jump-start my routines of spiritual observance. I say "called." I realize this could simply be the voice of my pietistic past, but it could also be God issuing an invitation. God has been more than a little confusing of late, and I take comfort in remembering the Bible records many prayers uttered in anger and despair, and the authors, we're led to believe, survived to tell about it. In this life on the edge, I have both more doubts and more desire: God seems more than ever a Mystery, and yet, also more than ever, I want to meet this Mystery. The only reason to be at the beach is to see the ocean. If I have neither the passion nor the altitude to dive deeply, I can at least wade in up to my knees. Who knows? If I survive that, I might try going out farther, up to my waist, maybe, or up to my chest. But I know what can happen: I won't have to be out far before the undertow pulls at my feet and suddenly I'll be in over my head and about then a large wave will plant my face in the sand. But can I just sit on my towel? Everything at the beach points to the water, everything moves toward it and is shaped by it; at the margins, the Mystery is the overwhelming fact, the sight and sound and smell and feel of an inescapable reality.

So with some trepidation, I will recover my routines of praying and meditating on Scripture and listening in the silence. Perhaps even attending church. I will show up, even if God doesn't. Or to give God the benefit of the doubt and to be honest about my own obtuseness, I should say I will show up even if I'm not aware of God's presence.

The last discipline I expect to find the most difficult. I'm not entirely certain I will follow through with it. During my last visit with my therapist, she said, "Don, the final thing I want to say to you is this: *the sacrifice of service.* That's all. I do not want to say anything more about it. Just remember these words."

I have remembered them, oh yes, the more so because I have tried to forget them. I've wanted to withdraw from people, be let alone to nurse my hurt feelings, like a dog going to a corner of the yard to be sick by himself. I've been excluded, and so in self-defense I've affirmed that exclusion and removed myself into a relatively solitary world.

But emotional masturbation may be, in the end, as sad and unsatisfying as the more famous kind. As important as it is to dive deeply into the mystery of ourselves, it may matter even more to throw ourselves into the problems of others. The self, in isolation from others, may be as insubstantial and transitory as a ghost, and the more we try to embrace it, the more we're left holding an emptiness, a solipsistic Nothing.

In Dan Wakefield's spiritual autobiography, he tells of his years of experience in psychoanalysis. The constant self-examination led him into a deep, dark pit. He comments, "I had gone into psychoanalysis to save myself, and at about the same time I went to East Harlem in the hope of helping others. Looking back from the vantage point of thirty years it seems quite clear in a literal way that what I did to save myself nearly killed me (I have never been so close to annihilation as I was in that extended waking nightmare at the end of analysis) and what I did in the hope of helping others nourished and sustained me and maybe even saved my life."[4]

My experience with psychoanalysis was not the nightmare it was for Wakefield. Indeed, I remain committed to the necessity of exploring personal depths. But I take his comments as fair warning: in isolation from others, this exploration will inevitably lead to dangerous distortion. We are relational creatures. Our existence is intimately connected with others. The healing of the soul will be unlikely unless we move attention away from ourselves to the needs of others. That's what my therapist was trying to say, I think.

I am making no promises, to God or myself. But I want to get ready, if possible. Feathers must be oiled. The nest must be prepared. There may be things I should do, even if I don't feel like it.

6

LETTING GO

Yesterday I ran along the beach, as per my resolution. It was beautiful: a summer day had cut to the head of the line to arrive in February, my legs and lungs seemed grateful for the outing, and the endorphins must have performed their happy science because my spirit brightened like the glare on the surf. Then I crawled out of bed this morning. My feet, in trying to haul me to the coffeepot, put up quite a fuss; they were so cranky you would have thought I had run barefoot on cement. Eventually I got hold of some Arabian Mocha Java and hobbled into my study to begin the day with prayer and meditation.

What happened next made walking into the kitchen look easy. About forty-five seconds into prayer, my thoughts wandered off like sheep in serious need of a Border collie. The perverse creatures went straight to the mud for a merry roll. Few things are as satisfying as anger directed toward someone you believe is particularly deserving. This morning that happened to be a certain Church official who has used every bureaucratic means to beat me down. I do not like this woman. Jesus told us to love our enemies, I realize, but I hope he gives us plenty of time to work this out. Thinking about her reminded me of her allies, such as the prosecuting attorney whose last words to the judicial commission were, "I ask you to return a verdict of 'guilty' or the entire body of Christ will be destroyed." *The entire body of Christ.*

Well, Lord, how dare I approach you in prayer—I who am the scum of the earth, worse than Nero and Hitler and Stalin (who simply caused a lot of damage but came nowhere near destroying your Church)? This brought to mind something I had read in a recent issue of *Time,* a quotation from a British commission studying foxhunting which said that the experience of being torn limb from limb by a pack of hounds "seriously compromises the welfare of the fox."[1] By then, as you see, my stream of consciousness had swelled into a river of resentment. So much for prayer and uplifting thoughts about God.

Holding *any* uplifting thought for more than a few seconds has been a challenge. Sitting at the beach, driving the car, lying in bed (especially at three A.M.), drinking morning coffee, sipping evening wine—times of rumination tend toward ruination. Guilt over things I've done, regret over opportunities I've wasted, sorrow over pain I've inflicted, anger at individuals who used me to unload their psychological baggage: a good many images and thoughts swirl around in a nasty stew that's hard to digest.

When a pelican bobs up from a dive, he has a mouthful that's impossible to digest. His pouch can carry three gallons and his stomach only one. William surfaces with an enormous sack under the bill filled with water and fish and God knows what else swimming and slithering. Gulls, the panhandlers of the beach, instantly appear to snatch his leftovers. You get the impression he needs a few moments to find his bearings, assess the situation, figure out what to do. Water spills out the top of the pouch and maybe spouts out a hole that had been torn by an unseen fishing hook. He has to manage a leaky mess while coming up with a strategy. He wants the biggest fish, but he'd also like to save the rest of the catch; he wants to store them in his esophagus without allowing any to escape or become dinner for Jonathan Livingston and his friends. Life is difficult and eventually reality will have its way: sooner or later, he has to squeeze out the excess water, letting go of both garbage and good things, in order to swallow at least one fish that will nourish him.

As I watch this, I feel a smile form, a chuckle erupt. Once in a while a pelican loses everything, and if I'm close enough, I'm sure I see an exasperation in his eyes. I imagine him thinking, "Damn! This is a tough way to get a dinner." It's classic comedy, up there with Charlie Chaplin slipping on a banana peel. Then it occurs to me that I, too, need to let go of some things I can neither carry nor swallow, and my laughter subsides. The comedy now seems a serious drama, even a tragedy.

About four years ago, before my work with Rachel, I was in therapy with Dr. O., a psychiatrist who knew I needed to sojourn in a painful place. She had enough wisdom and courage and patience not to lift me out of my problems but to keep me standing in dark corners of my personality and past. Our sessions together were often tumultuous. It was not easy returning to my office to play the role of president-in-charge-of-the-situation when I felt very much the president-out-of-control. So I adopted a routine to help with the transition: I would drive to Sausalito for an hour or two of oiling the teak on my boat.

Teak! A wonder of the world, a wood of warmth and beauty and amazing durability. What I like best about it is this: it witnesses to the possibility of redemption. Be it ever so weatherworn and wayward, the right oil restores it like the breath of God blowing into Ezekiel's dry bones. And teak oil! A golden elixir, a wondrous marriage of divine creativity and human ingenuity. To feel it on your fingers, warmed by a summer sun, translucent and silken, lubricating and sliding and penetrating—well, it's more than a sensuous delight; it's creative, it's life-giving. Rub it into wood and you become a god, you call Lazarus from the tomb, you usher the dead into resurrection. You should be required to spend years as a novitiate before being allowed near such power.

But first, the teak must be prepared. That's the hard part, and that's what I did after my psychotherapy sessions. I would brush on oil remover—a mysterious concoction so potent it should probably be illegal—and then watch it go to work: as if by magic, the old, sour, dark oil would bubble to the surface, and then I would wipe it off. I would brush on a second coat, to make sure I had gotten it all out, and yet another if necessary, and each time I would wipe off the ugliness, and I knew I was wiping away more than old oil when tears started flowing down my cheeks. I was wiping away the darkness inside me rising to the surface, the old hurts and angers and guilt and resentments.

And then came the conclusion of the sacrament, done with a prayer. I would take new, clean teak oil, and I would rub it into the wood, working it deeply into the grain and the cracks, and I would watch as the wood got up and walked out of the tomb, and I would say, "Please, God . . ."

There is pleasure, not often acknowledged, in dark thoughts and ugly feelings. If anger has its rewards, so do misunderstandings and resentments and hatreds and—best of all—the belief that one is a victim. They energize me with self-righteousness and wrap me in the warm embrace of self-pity. They create an identity, actually, help define me, and I am afraid to let go of them. What will fill the emptiness? This fear was expressed well in one of Saul Bellow's novels: *"To tell the truth, I never had it so good,* he wrote. *But I lack the strength of character to bear such joy.* That was hardly a joke. When a man's breast feels like a cage from which all the dark birds have flown—he is free, he is light. And he longs to have his vultures back again. He wants his customary struggles, his nameless, empty works, his anger, his afflictions, and his sins."[2]

One blustery Sunday afternoon in Edinburgh, Scotland, I walked up Arthur's Seat, the hill overlooking the city. As I rounded the face of the rock cliff, I noticed a young woman looking up. My eyes followed her, and I saw, about halfway to the summit, her boyfriend hanging in frozen panic. His fingers and toes had each found a tenuous grip and his cheek was pressed against the stone. He couldn't move.

I took one look at the vertical rock, and I decided this was no time for heroics. I was about to run for help when I saw the heads of two policemen peering over the top ledge. They told him to stay put, an entirely unnecessary command, and they assured him they would be right back. They returned with a thick rope, which they tossed over the side and maneuvered to within a few inches of him.

He knew what to do. He needed to grasp the rope; that would be his salvation. But he did not move. How could he? He would have to defy all logic, rebel against every instinct in his body, and let go of the cliff. His circumstances were uncomfortable, to be sure, but he was still alive, and who knew what would happen if he let go? The rock was scraping his skin, his muscles were weary, and he was afraid, very afraid, and now he had to do the hardest thing in his life. He had to risk death to find life.

He waited a long time until he found the courage to do what he had to do, and when he did, he was pulled to safety.

. . . .

What if you lose all the fish out of your pouch? What if you leave the wood barren and dry? What if you fall from your one, albeit dangerous, purchase on reality? Letting go leaves you at risk, vulnerable.

Along the water's edge I've been seeing empty casings of the *Panulirus interruptus,* which is not a method of birth control but the official term for the California spiny lobster. Almost every day at the beach, during the last few months, I've observed these dark red shells. It's made me curious. I've never noticed them before. In consulting my books, I discover that lobsters, from time to time, shed their exoskeletons. It's necessary, apparently, for the growth process. They need shells to protect them from being torn apart, and yet, as a result of having grown on the inside, the shell must be abandoned. If they did not cast it off, it would soon become a prison—and finally, a casket.

The danger for lobsters is the brief period between discarding the old shell and forming a new one. Lobsters are terribly vulnerable, exposed to powerful currents and hungry schools of fish. Sometimes they die between shells. There is serious risk in throwing off the old, but what choice do they have? The alternative is certain death: the old shell would slowly suffocate them.

There was a period when Miles Davis, the great trumpeter, lost the sound of music. Something within him died. But then he started producing a new sound—what musicians call "cool jazz," which was a significant contribution to the development of this art form. Something inside Davis died; there was emptiness and darkness. Then out of the inner chaos a new thing was created.

. . . .

Letting go of bitterness and resentment is difficult because these dark emotions often protect us from the terror of losing more cherished possessions. As long as I'm busily angry at the aforementioned Church bureaucrat, I can avoid facing more painful losses. My imaginary conversations with her, filled with devastating wit and withering put-downs, distract me from what her scheming suggests: I have lost respect and influence. If I let go of anger today, I will be left with the much harder task of letting go of my identity tomorrow.

This is the raw, throbbing nerve of my distress, the source of much fear. The painful things that have happened in the last year testify, with harsh clarity, that I must relinquish an image I have shaped and polished for many years. I was a beloved pastor, an influential leader, a respected colleague. Now who am I? In our culture, what you *do* helps define who you *are*, especially if you're a man. Your work locates you in the social world and assigns value to you and is a reference point for self-understanding. It's easy to argue that this shouldn't be the case, but centuries of sociological conditioning have hard-wired us this way. Preachers may wax eloquent in proclaiming that our worth comes from God and not our achievements, and of course they're right. But if they were kicked out of the pulpit, what would they feel in their guts, in that place of instinct far removed from careful theological reasoning? They would feel stripped and embarrassingly naked.

When I lost my job I also lost a seminary-owned car. So I had to go through the awful process of buying a new one. In my first test-drive, as we headed out of the lot, the salesman turned to me and said, "So what do you do for a living?" I was wholly dumbfounded, shaken to the core of my being; I became a blithering idiot. I had no idea what to tell him. I couldn't bring myself to say *Nothing,* because that would be like saying *I am nothing.* So I made up something about being "in transition with my career." Yeah, the way a car being smashed by a train is in transition.

Actually, what I must release has already been taken from me. Letting go means surrendering to the reality of my situation, allowing a realignment of my internal and external worlds. This demands honest truth-telling and unflinching dedication to reality—dangerous work for which there seems to be no immediate reward. Every act of letting go is a loss of control, a personal divestment, a relinquishment toward the unknown, and in this sense, a step toward death. Corpses don't cling to anything.

But I am beginning to understand that not all deaths are the same. There are two kinds, and sometimes we have a choice between them: one leads only to nothingness, absolute dissolution; another leads through emptiness to a different life. I'm tempted to say *richer life* or *better life* (as a Christian who clings to the hope of resurrection), but whether that proves true in my present existence—next year, say, or next decade—it is too soon to say. Things may or may not turn out for the better. Nonetheless, there does seem to be a death you can live with, or perhaps better stated, a death you can't live without. It's shucking off a lobster's shell; it's saying the last rites for something inside Miles Davis; it's descending into the Inferno to reach Paradisio.

The most painful death I must enter, the one I am struggling to avoid with a fear that is nearly panic, is the relationship I have had with my daughters. I love them as deeply as any parent loves his or her children, which is to say, with a love often blind and selfish but nonetheless about as pure as humans manage this side of heaven. I have wanted the best for them; I have wanted to protect them from suffering; I have wanted to nurture them toward spiritual maturity. But then another love of mine, misbegotten and misdirected, bestowed on them enormous pain. I betrayed not only my ex-wife but my children, too. I was neither the father they thought I was, nor the one I aspired to be. In the darkness of early morning I often see their eyes, still those of children, looking up with confusion and questions. I want to hold them in an embrace that will magically erase wrong choices and bind broken hearts and earn new respect.

When I talk with them now, I struggle to find the right words, the explanations to ease misunderstanding and move toward a renewed relationship. I'm working hard at this, with earnest intensity, but this labor, I'm ashamed to admit, is really an attempt to control them. I want them to respond to me in certain ways; I want them to have new esteem for me; I want them to see not only my failures but my strengths; I want them to be grateful for the good things I have done. And yes, the use of the first person singular pronoun in the last sentence signals the selfishness of my attempt to force my desires upon them. I can see that I haven't let go of them.

A challenge of parenthood, even in the best of circumstances, is learning how to let go of your children. It's part of the bargain: you bring them into life and pour your love into them and worry over them and pray for them—so one day they can walk away from you. And you feel good about most of the steps they take into the larger world, you really do, but all the same, it hurts more than you ever imagined when you were taking Lamaze classes and painting the nursery.

How could you ever be prepared for watching your sixteen-year-old drive off in the car for the first time? Jennifer and I had spent many hours lurching and jerking our way through the parking lot of the Del Mar racetrack until she gradually gained confidence behind the wheel. On her sixteenth birthday she was examined by the Department of Motor Vehicles, and to my surprise and disappointment, passed with high marks. That meant one terrible, awful, miserable thing: she could now drive off by herself.

So that afternoon we stood together in the driveway but were on two different planets; she was in High Excitement and I was in Utter Anxiety. I gave her the keys, hoping she wouldn't notice my quivering hand and sweating forehead. She said, "Thanks, Dad," as if it were no big deal, as if she weren't actually getting in the car and driving alone onto dangerous streets into a more dangerous world, as if she weren't passing a transition toward adulthood when she would drive by herself along many roads I would not travel, as if she weren't forcing me to let go of her and thus, in a way, let go of part of myself. I stood on the curb and watched her drive away, and as the car got smaller and a lump in my throat grew larger, I knew it had nothing to do with her driving.

I was saying good-bye to her. I've always hated saying good-bye, even watching others do it. Walking through an airport, with little dramas of farewell enacted all around me, plunges me into an ambivalent reverie. On the one hand, a faint envy floats just below the surface of my consciousness, only occasionally rising into awareness. Each painful separation, with tearful embraces and prolonged kisses, witnesses to a bond of affection that resists being broken, and being human seems never more glorious. On the other hand, these partings also conjure darker spirits. They remind me of the transitoriness of life, that glory always brings with it tragedy, that life takes place between homecoming and separation, gain and loss, love and pain. In each good-bye I catch a whiff of bouquets, but too many, like the scent of a funeral home.

So the only sensible thing is to hold as tightly as possible and never let go. The moment of release could be the moment of loss. *Will* be the moment of loss. But what choice do we have?

What can I do but allow my daughters to be the grown women they are? What can I do but trust that as they drive away from me they will find the road toward a forgiveness I have no right to demand, a healing only God can provide, and a joy in the future that will overwhelm the sorrows of the past? What can I do but renew the promise their mother and I made at their baptisms, to entrust them to the grace and good providence of God? What can I do but let go, and hope that this death will lead beyond itself to a renewed relationship in the freedom of mature love?

What will William and his mate feel when, ten or twelve weeks after their offspring hatch, they stop bringing fish to the nest? Catching enough for the family has kept them busy. Three chicks would require six to nine pounds of fish each day. Parents must feel some relief when this responsibility has concluded, not unlike human counterparts who write the final check for college tuition. But do they feel anything else? Do they have emotions that break when seeing the eyes of chicks, born of their flesh, looking at them in disbelief and hunger?

Legend has it that mother pelicans care so much for their young that, if they are starving, they will readily sacrifice themselves. "For everything there is a season," the preacher of Ecclesiastes said, "a time to embrace and a time to refrain from embracing; a time to seek, and a time to lose; a time to keep, and a time to throw away."[3] A season of necessary loss may come, a time of letting go, but what must be in a heart that would give itself for food when it must walk away and force chicks out of the nest, abandon them to a dangerous, self-taught course in survival as they learn how to swim and fly and fish on their own? I do not know. I only know there is no other way.

7

GUANO ON THE HEAD

When a pelican surfaces from a dive, pouch filled and squirming, the poor bird is not allowed to dine in peace. Before excess water can be squeezed out, along with fish that can't be swallowed, visitors arrive to crash the party.

Gulls.

I know of no one who likes them, except Mormons. The state bird of Utah, oddly enough, is the California gull. The bird came to the rescue in 1848 by eating grasshoppers that were devouring crops. This act of charity, performed with substantial self-interest, may be the only in gull history, and the followers of Joseph Smith have ever after expressed gratitude. For others, however, the gull is a low-life: scavenger, garbage picker, overhead screecher, and general nuisance. My mother still gets agitated when telling about an afternoon, many years ago, when she was sunbathing and one turned her bare midriff into a privy. You rarely hear someone say, "Oh, look, a beautiful gull."

I have an affinity, especially these days, for outcasts. So I try to be kind to the creatures, rushing to their defense whenever possible. I point out the beauty of white feathers; I describe their actions as "playful"; I've been known to throw them bread crusts. My friends consider me a bleeding-heart liberal.

But if I were a pelican, I wouldn't be so tolerant. When gulls see a pouch full of water—and thus maybe fish—they transcend their own considerable rudeness by hovering and fluttering about, shamelessly trying to steal part of the catch. They will even sit on the poor bird's head, whether resting from thievery or awaiting further opportunity for mischief, I don't know. It's quite a sight, really: a gull perched on the head of a pelican, as if it were his appointed place, as if it were a fine thing to be relieving himself of his last dinner, crapping down the recently groomed feathers beneath him. After watching a few moments of this, I want the pelican to strike back, to teach the pests a lesson or two. That's what I would do, make no mistake about it. I would use those hard mandibles as effective weapons, smacking and whacking and administering justice. If a few heads got cracked, it would serve them right.

So much for mushy liberalism.

But a being can take only so much. It's hard enough to manage the challenges of life without the harassment of those who feed off your difficulties. That's what I'm telling myself as I picture gulls hovering around my head: the Church leader who used me to vent resentment of her own husband's unfaithfulness; faculty members eager to get even with a president who had threatened their power; closet adulterers channeling their own guilt toward me; former "friends" who have disappeared; and one gull, the largest, most aggressive in the flock, who bears a striking resemblance to me. I want these images to fly away, to quit casting a shadow around me. But what I really want is to set the record straight, to tell the *whole* truth, to strike back.

I have not been able to do this, of course. My every move is scrutinized by individuals and committees to determine whether I'm really repentant, whether I'm ready for admission back into Church leadership. Rarely does anyone actually speak with me, presumably because this might disrupt the preferred flow of information: someone makes an idle comment, perhaps in ignorance, which becomes gossip, which grows into rumor, which gets accepted as "fact." I'm in the classic "damned if I do and damned if I don't" situation. If I respond, I'm considered defensive; if I keep quiet, I'm arrogant. If I express anger, I'm not truly sorry; if I bite my tongue, I'm in denial. A couple years ago, some in my former congregation were saying I didn't understand the hurt I had caused, but when I offered to meet with them to express my sorrow, I was accused of meddling and being manipulative. At my trial one witness for the prosecution warned the judicial commission to beware of anything I might say, because I am a preacher who is smooth with words; she also said that if I stumble in my testimony and cry (which I did), I would be "playing to the camera." It seems that anything I do or say will be used against me, and this makes me want to strike all the harder at gulls.

Then I watch the pelicans. Do you know what they do to the gulls? Nothing. They do not swing at them. They do not shake their heads. They do not grumble complaints. They do not seem annoyed, even in the slightest. They do *nothing*. "The brown pelican," one ornithologist wrote, "is a pacifist of the bird world, epitomizing a spirit of peaceful live-and-let-live coexistence."[1]

Is this why they have no natural enemies?

Is this their secret of survival for forty million years?

The only way for me to respond like a pelican is to change something on the inside: I must find a place of calm at the center of my being, a place from which peace can flow outward toward my relations with others. How can I do this?

The answer, I know, is forgiveness. I have delivered countless sermons on this theme, and I have often recommended it in counseling sessions as a necessary step toward healing. Now I need to listen to my preaching and heed my advice. Frankly, I wish it were not so; forgiveness is difficult, always a painful and astonishing achievement. But I'm beginning to realize it's not simply a gift I extend to others but a gift I offer myself, the only way I can let go of the resentment and bitterness, the only way to serenity.

As I run along the beach today, with the distant line between deep blue sea and light blue sky as sharp as it can be on a day following rain, I ask myself, "What if I were so free of inner agitation that I could give myself fully to the beauty around me?" It is suddenly as clear as the horizon that the first to benefit from forgiveness would be me. If I can surrender the right to get even, and in my heart, at least, extend an olive branch to those who have wounded me, I will free myself from feelings that, in the end, do more harm to me than to anyone else. Anger, resentment, and hatred devour the soul and even destroy the body.

How can I not forgive others? I'm hoping others grant me this gift of release. I need it more than anyone. I have no right to demand forgiveness, but I have asked for it and am praying for it. That some have not been willing to grant it is part of what has hurt me and made me want to strike back—and yes, I see the incongruity in this.

More to the point, I'm counting on the forgiveness of God. Whatever faith I have clings to this one hope: the God I have served for many years, however imperfectly, is a God of grace. This has been the foundation of my Christian beliefs. If I am correct, nothing else really matters; God's acceptance should sweep away, like a flood tide, the scattered debris of human condemnation. And if I am wrong, well, again, nothing else matters; if God is not forgiving and not working for good in all this, why should I care about anything else?

One Sunday, as a young pastor, I was leading the congregation in saying the Lord's Prayer. For some reason, I skipped over the phrase "forgive us our debts as we forgive our debtors." I went straight from "give us this day our daily bread" to "lead us not into temptation." As I blasted this boo-boo through the microphone there was an awkward pause and the unmistakable sound of stifled snickers. It's not every day you hear a pastor botch something any Sunday school child knows. I've since wondered if my mistake signaled an unconscious discomfort with this part of the prayer. I'm willing and eager to pray for my own forgiveness, to be sure, but linking it to my forgiving others is more than a little disturbing.

If I can't forgive others, it may be because I haven't forgiven myself. You don't have to be Sigmund Freud to know that until you release yourself from failure and break the wagging finger of self-accusation, you will find it difficult, maybe impossible, to forgive others. I have projected my self-condemnation onto others, and their negative judgments have thus had a power over me, a power to wound and make me defensive.

I've been seeing myself at the beach, standing at the water's edge. But actually I've been huddled in a cave carved by the sharp edge of my guilt in sandstone cliffs. I'm going to have to crawl out into a larger world, a world that reaches across the Mystery to a future horizon and one filled with other people. Forgiveness is not overlooking wrongs, or excusing them, or forgetting them. It is necessary precisely because something can't be overlooked or excused or forgotten. It may be the only remedy left for me.

There is a Jewish folktale about an otter who rushed before the king crying, "My lord, you are one who loves justice and rules fairly. You have established peace among all your creatures, and yet there is no peace."

"Who has broken the peace?" asked the king.

"The Weasel! I dove into the water to hunt food for my children, leaving them in the care of the Weasel. While I was gone my children were killed. 'An eye for an eye,' the Good Book says. I demand vengeance!"

The king sent for the Weasel, who soon appeared before him. "You have been charged with the death of the Otter's children. How do you plead?" demanded the king.

"Alas, my lord," wept the Weasel, "I am responsible for the death of the Otter's children, though it was clearly an accident. As I heard the Woodpecker sound the danger alarm, I rushed to defend our land. In doing so I trampled the Otter's children by accident."

The king summoned the Woodpecker. "Is it true that you sounded the alarm with your mighty beak?" inquired the king.

"It is true, my lord," replied the Woodpecker. "I began the alarm when I spied the Scorpion sharpening his dagger."

When the Scorpion appeared before the king, he was asked if he indeed had sharpened his dagger. "You understand that sharpening your dagger is an act of war?" asked the king.

"I understand," said the Scorpion, "but I prepared only because I observed the Turtle polishing his armor."

In his defense the Turtle said, "I would not have polished my armor had I not seen the Crab preparing his sword."

The Crab declared, "I saw the Lobster swinging its javelin."

When the Lobster appeared before the king, he explained, "I began to swing my javelin when I saw the Otter swimming toward my children, ready to devour them."

Turning to the Otter, the king announced, "You, not the Weasel, are the guilty party. The blood of your children is upon your head. Whoever sows death shall reap it."[2]

·   ·   ·   ·

I am guilty. My actions have initiated a cycle of spiritual violence. I want to do what I can to end it. If it means forgiving those who have hurt me, then forgiveness it must be. Others may be too wounded to return the gift, at least for the time being. Moreover, institutional processes are at work, with their own energy and momentum, and these will have to be played out. For my part, though, I want to be forgiving. At least, this is my resolution today. I am motivated, to a degree, by self-interest. I can imagine what it would be like: the deep-down release, the peaceful oblivion to annoying gulls, the freedom of living on a broader expanse of the beach. But all this might be similar to a drunk's tearful speeches to bar mates; in the morning, things may feel different. It may be dangerous to make bold declarations under the influence of an intoxicating idea. For now, though, I want this as much as anything, and I'm going to assume the desire will remain come the sobering light of a new day.

But how do I do it? That's the crucial question. *How can I forgive?* I've been searching through my books (a pastor has many on this subject), but I'm not finding much help. The problem is, as I try to get the recommended steps fixed in my mind, I'm reminded that others need to forgive me, and that makes me think of my own failures, and then I feel unworthy of any forgiveness—and before I know it I'm back in my cave.

Perhaps the first step toward forgiveness is focusing on something else, something other than my resentments. The way to ignore the gulls is to stay attentive to the fish in my pouch. The Purple Lizard Principle might be relevant here. If I tell you to quit thinking about purple lizards—just stop, banish them from your awareness!—the little buggers will crawl all over your thoughts. And the harder you try, the more they will proliferate: they will soon be crawling up and down the walls of your consciousness, covering every square inch of your imagination. The only way to forget about purple lizards is to think about something else.

I need to let go of some things, as I said in the last chapter. Nice theory, tough in practice. The harder I try, the firmer my troubled thoughts grip me—and with them my anger and resentment and sorrow. So my hope is this: I must think about something else. As the Apostle puts it, "If there is any excellence and if there is anything worthy of praise, think about these things."[3] There is my wife, to begin with. And my daughters. And my parents. And news that I'm going to be a grandfather. And making plans for the future. And books, the novels and poetry, that have always transported me into another world. And, of course, pelicans.

Getting busy with other things is not the same as forgiveness, I know. But it might help make it possible. It might be like digging out the beach between Del Mar and Solana Beach. Sand had accumulated and closed off the lagoon from the ocean. This blocked the tidal flow, and without cleansing flushes, the lagoon choked. It became a fetid, dying bog. So a few months ago the authorities decided to dredge a new opening to enable the ocean, with its lunar comings and goings, to administer healing. Disciplining myself to think about other things, offering gratitude for all that remains, may be like a shovel that opens me so the Mystery can flow in with cleansing power.

The Mystery will have to flow in, I'm sure. There needs to be a cleansing power to drain and reinvigorate the lagoon of my life. The irony of my situation is that my "cure"—the psychotherapy, the investigation and trial, the Church "discipline" that ordered exclusion—has had the effect of turning me inward, isolating me, forcing me into self-absorption and self-protectiveness—and in the end, all this fosters the very self-centeredness that got me into trouble in the first place. It's as though I've been sent to a hospital where I've inevitably caught a worse, more dangerous infection. The disease has been treated, but at what cost? I'm a self-enclosed lagoon; the seawater is evaporating and what remains is filled with death. The result is that I feel powerless to do the one thing I need to do, which is to forgive—forgive myself and forgive others.

I need the Mystery to flow into the lagoon. If God is a forgiving deity—the One whose Spirit was in Jesus, who, when nailed to a cross, prayed, "Father, forgive them, for they do not know what they are doing"[4]—then I need God to do for me what I cannot do on my own. While Martin Niemöller was in Hitler's prison, he wrote, "It took me a long time to learn that God is not the enemy of my enemies. He is not even the enemy of His enemies."[5] God has already forgiven, indeed loves, my enemies, and now I need God to do it through me, to help me to do what, from a human perspective, is unnatural, even absurd, and yet entirely necessary. Perhaps then I can be as peaceful as a pelican with gulls on his head.

FLYING TOGETHER

By yesterday afternoon I was ready to forgive every gull that had ever crapped on my head. Overcome by a conviction of God's forgiveness for me and for everyone else, I wanted to do my part by offering complete absolution to everyone who had ever hurt me. I knew it would take a while; it would not be easy releasing some people and wishing them well. But that was my goal, that's where I was headed. Let a thousand gulls swarm around me, I would be a pelican, and a mighty fine one at that.

Then came Walt's call. Walt is my official "liaison" with the Presbytery of San Francisco, a dear man who models the best of pastoral compassion. He wanted to tell me about a meeting that had been held to discuss my case. His first halting words signaled that things had not gone well.

This should not have surprised me.

Whenever I make a bold commitment to improve in some area of my life, I'm immediately put to the test. If I determine to be more patient, say, I will endure, before the day is over, enough snarled traffic and surly sales clerks and intrusive telemarketers to stomp to death whatever seedling I had planted. If I promise to be a gentler man, within hours—count on it—my wife will do something to trigger my irritation. I'm not sure why I ever make resolutions; it's an invitation to trouble. So after deciding to be forgiving, I should have expected the Presbytery to do something that would make me want to swat a few gulls.

And I should have expected it for another reason: there are too many forces at work to expect a resolution of my ecclesiastical troubles anytime soon. The constitution of my denomination says that discipline is "for redeeming, not for punishing. It should be exercised as a dispensation of mercy and not of wrath."[1] I have learned to understand this as a statement of lofty aspiration rather than a promise of actual policy. The Church is an institution with sociopsychological dynamics that sometimes crash into its theological convictions.

I have been trying to understand why the Presbytery chose to ignore all that I had done to make things right during the last six years—my confession and repentance, the attempts at restitution, the years of psychotherapy. My theory is that to take any of this seriously would leave no way to punish me. Although the Church is committed to mercy, it wants to get in plenty of hard licks against actual sinners before it reaches that goal.

There are reasons for this. Punishment is more than a desire to strike back, more than a vengeful reaction to make the wrongdoer pay for the hurt he or she has caused. It is this, certainly; the instinct springs so suddenly and unbidden it seems to rise from the depths of our unconscious, as I can attest from my own feelings toward those who have hurt me. But the impulse to punish has other, more complex motives behind it.

My failure was not simply a personal matter. I was in a leadership role, a position of trust and authority. When my adultery became public, there is a sense in which *all* trust and authority was undermined. So the institution had to protect itself by demonstrating its intolerance for such behavior; it had to say, in effect, we've thrown out the bad apple so you will be safe with the rest in the box.

Moreover, there is the matter of psychological transference. In the words of Ernest Becker, "groups 'use' the leader sometimes with little regard for him personally, but always with regard to fulfilling their own needs and urges."[2] When I was a pastor and seminary president, the spiritual ambitions of many people were projected onto me (*If he can be that good of a Christian, maybe I can, too*), and this meant I was often elevated, set up on the proverbial pedestal of admiration. And when I fell, transference continued to happen, only now in a mirror-image reversal: the deep anxieties of many people were projected onto me (*If he can fail sexually, maybe I can, too*), and thus I had to be banished from the community, like the scapegoat made to carry a load of sin into the wilderness. It recently occurred to me that I never complained when people projected too many good things onto me, so why should I whine if they now project too many bad things onto me? If I happily received the one, I had better be willing to take the other. I chose what might be called the public anonymity of leadership, after all; I took on a role that would elicit a response to my position rather than my person. I had best accept this as part of the cost.

So the Church, as an institution, had to find a public means of expiating my sin. This is why, I think, the investigating committee and the judicial commission seemed so little interested in my repentance. If it were simply a matter of sin and repentance, they are good enough theologians—they're Presbyterians!—to know they would have to forgive and restore me. So they fled to the *real* religion of our time: by ignoring the counseling I had received, they could punish me by forcing me to undergo psychotherapy.

Now, I greatly appreciate psychotherapy, as this book makes clear. I'm just not keen on it as a form of punishment. At one point, one of my therapists said, "Don, you're not sick. You're a

sinner. Why can't the Church deal with that? Isn't that the business it's in?"

"Well, yes," I replied, "that's its *theological* business, but as a
human institution, it has to work through a lot of other stuff to
get there."

I offer all this not to minimize my wrongdoing but to under-
score its seriousness. My offense was not simply against individuals; I hurt an organization—an organization I have loved deeply.
It's now trying to stumble toward some kind of healing.

Understanding these things, however, does not ease my pain.
I can step back, at times, and I can see why there was perhaps an
"inevitability" to what transpired, why the Church has "had" to
do certain things, why its official judgment of me has been about
much more than me as a person. Nonetheless, I can't escape me-
as-a-person; I can't get out of my own skin. *I* have been condemned. All the philosophizing in the world can't close the
bleeding wound of being rejected, cast out.

I'm at the beach again, waiting. Where are the pelicans today?
Were they told to stay away from me? Don't get near Serious Sinner, William.

Eventually, three appear on my right. They are soaring about
thirty feet high. Suddenly, as though in response to an air-traffic
controller, they descend in union to skim along the crest of a breaking wave. They fly in single file, wingtips about an inch from the
water. They have the Right Stuff, that's obvious: Charles Lindbergh and Chuck Yeager and Neil Armstrong gliding home. I envy
their relaxed excellence, their obvious peace.

I wish I were with them, I say to myself, realizing I have em-
phasized the word *them*. I wish I were with *them,* part of the

squadron, on the team, one of the guys; I wish I could join them at the rookery for a drink after we landed.

Brown pelicans are almost always together. You rarely see them alone. They are highly gregarious, doing everything in community: they build nests together, they rear chicks together, they preen together, they sit in the sun together, they swim together, they dive together, they fish together, and they fly together.

Yes, they fly together. They use the common V-formation of many species or an angled slash line (/). They fly close to each other, for good reason. The pelican ahead lowers wind resistance, making less power necessary for those behind and creating a turbulence that provides extra lift. (The same principle is at work when a bicyclist uses the draft of the rider in front of him or a race car driver stays close behind a competitor.) The leader has a tough go of it, of course, and must work harder to maintain speed. But they rotate positions, allowing the leader to drop back to the middle to rest as a new one takes his or her place.

I have never yet seen a perfectly neat formation. They always fly with a kind of ragged elegance, and I've often wanted to blow a whistle and bark a few commands to get them into line (I'm still a Presbyterian). Recently, though, I've begun to appreciate their utilitarian approach: the community is for mutual support, not for show; they are more interested in results than following rules of order.

The community flying above me intensifies my loneliness. I am walking alone on this beach, and I know I'm walking not only toward Batiquitos Lagoon but toward a full-blown extravaganza of self-pity. But something is holding me back. Memories are coming from somewhere, altogether too positive for my mood. They are so startling, I decide to pay attention.

I recall a session with Rachel, my therapist, as my trial was drawing near. She told me about a friend of hers who discovered, while doing research in South Africa, an unusual way of administering justice. In the Babemba tribe, a person who has acted irresponsibly or done something wrong is placed in the center of the village, alone and unfettered. All work ceases, and all the men, women, and children gather in a large circle around the accused. Then each person, one by one, speaks to him about all the good things he has done in his lifetime. Yes, the *good* things. Every incident, every experience that can be recalled, is recounted with as much accuracy as possible. All positive attributes, generous deeds, strengths, and kindnesses are recited carefully and at length. No one is permitted to fabricate, or exaggerate, or be facetious. This ceremony often lasts several days and does not cease until everyone is drained of every positive comment that can be made about the person in question. Then the circle is broken, a joyous celebration takes place, and the person is welcomed back into the tribe.

My immediate response to Rachel came out of bitterness. "Let's hope," I said, "the Christian missionaries don't get to them!" I felt as though a circle had formed around me, to be sure, but they were throwing stones, not affirmation.

A few days later I was talking with my buddy Woody. We had met in college but didn't become close until seminary. We were an unlikely duo: he had hair to his shoulders, I had it neatly trimmed; he wore jeans and sandals, I wore khakis and penny loafers; he worked to end the Vietnam War, I worked for A's; he knew the plight of migrant workers, I knew the declension of Greek verbs; he had a voice that sounded like God, I had a voice reminiscent of wind blowing through a hole in the wall. Deep friendships can't really be explained, any more than you can explain a Mozart sonata.

Now he pastors a large congregation two states away. Our conversations are mostly on the telephone, but that doesn't inhibit us: we laugh and cry and vent anger and discuss weighty matters. When I told him the secret of my adultery and the storm that was about to break, he said, "Well, I love you, brother, and I am committed to you, no matter what happens. It will probably get messy, with plenty of suffering down the road. But you can count on this: either you will be preaching at my funeral or I will be preaching at yours."

So I was telling Woody about the Babemba tribe, and as I spoke, a lump grew in my throat, which soon became the size of a watermelon, and I couldn't even choke out the last few sentences. I was overwhelmed with the image of such unmerited mercy, of such affirmation from the community. I could feel, for an instant, how the person in the middle of the circle would be overwhelmed by grace, and that grace would judge and redeem and restore to the community all at once. I wanted that for myself. I seemed to be undergoing something very different.

"What a strange idea," I said with sarcasm. "A community that responds in grace. Imagine that." But even as I said it, I felt a sudden clash within, as though I had just played a false note, as though I had set myself at odds with a deeper truth. When I hung up the telephone, I sat for a few minutes, and in the silence I seemed to hear a voice saying, *You've been so focused on those throwing stones, you haven't been grateful enough for those throwing support. You, too, have a circle of grace around you.* I saw Woody standing there, telling me that my failure was not the most important thing in my life, and that our friendship would endure. And Woody wasn't alone. My parents were there; despite great sorrow, they never relaxed their embrace of love. And Bob, first my lawyer and then a close friend and partner in my travails. And Scott and Maureen and Dottie and Walt and Kathy and Carol and Arnold. . . .

I no longer feel quite so alone as I walk down this beach. A little crowd is with me, and it seems to be gaining size and strength. A smile forms on my face as I remember the first words of the chairman of the seminary board after I had confessed to him. He said with his east Texas drawl, "Well, Don, I don't want this to come as a shock to you, but I always knew you were a sinner."

And I hear Frank's voice in the crowd. He's my friend with a wooden leg and an optimism that would embarrass Robert Schuller. He is always calling to see how I'm doing. "What's happening. You all right? You know how much I love you? God used you to help turn my life around, and there is nothing I wouldn't do for you. *Absolutely nothing.*" I believe him. I picture him in Korea, racing back to a barn to rescue one of his wounded men, a barn he knew the North Koreans had targeted, and I hear the explosion that left his leg and his future a long way from home. Now that I'm wounded and the rockets are flying toward me, he's limping back to rescue me, and if necessary he would sacrifice his remaining leg to save me.

Some years ago my family and I were vacationing in Seattle. On our last day I wanted to sail once more on Lake Union. The wind was blowing. *Really* blowing, as in trees bent parallel to the ground, as in water churning with angry whitecaps, as in not a single boat out there. Standing at the end of the dock, I decided I had neither the skill nor the courage to attempt it. Then I heard a voice behind me, the owner of the rental company. She said, "Well, I don't usually let boats go out on a day like this, but I've seen you sail. You can probably handle it." Whereupon my pride took over and trampled my good sense.

About ten seconds away from the dock, I knew I had done something very, very stupid. The little fourteen-foot Lido was about to go over. I didn't actually imagine myself getting killed, only because I was too busy trying to stay alive. I crawled forward to lower the mainsail, and with only the jib managed to turn back. Nearing the dock, I saw the owner standing there, and next to her a man who, I later learned, had come by to reserve a boat for the weekend.

"What's the matter?" she hollered at me.

"I can't do it!"

She said something to the man next to her, who appeared to be an Asian American businessman, and then said to me, "He'll go with you!"

He was in a white shirt and tie, slacks, and oxford shoes. I was not seized with confidence.

"Does he know what he's doing?" I asked.

She nodded and he nodded. I didn't know what to do but invite him aboard. He loosened his tie and slipped off his shoes, and a few seconds later we were rocketing across Lake Union. We were both "hiked out"—holding a line for dear life and bracing our feet (his in socks) on the edge of the boat and leaning as far back as possible, our butts just a few feet from the water, waves crashing over us. His white shirt was plastered to his body. He laughed and said, "This is great! I don't know how I'm going to explain this at the office, but who cares? What a blast!"

It was. Of the hundreds of sailing adventures I've had, this was one of the best. The adrenaline-pumping, white-knuckle-producing, heart-pounding thrill of the ride, and the unexpected fellowship, the partnership formed against the elements.

I couldn't have done it on my own, that's a fact. The wind was too strong, too overpowering, and the boat would have capsized.

I might have drowned. I needed help; I needed another to lend weight and skill to keep me upright.

The memories are growing noisier than the gulls scolding a surf fisherman who refuses to share his bait. I now sense a small army of support all around me. Greg is there, leaning against the door-jamb of my seminary office. We had just been in a faculty meeting, the worst ever, and that's saying something. I had had to confess my failures and tell them about the Presbytery investigation, and they had made speeches, as faculty are wont to do, and they asked questions that were impossible to answer.

When I returned to my office, my head dropped onto my desk and I sobbed uncontrollably. I felt utterly alone. Then came a knock at the door. In walked Greg, holding up a couple of Heinekens. I could only nod. We sat drinking in silence, not knowing what to say. To this day I can still savor that beer, best I ever had. It tasted a lot like bread and wine.

And Peggy is there, walking again on the beach as she had done for so many years at Del Mar with a funny straw hat shading her black skin. A few months ago she telephoned and asked if she could visit.

"Yes, that would be nice," I said. "When would you like to come over?"

"Right now."

"Ah, I suppose that would be fine."

When she arrived she explained that she had gotten up from the breakfast table to get more cereal when she heard God say, *Call Don and Shari.* "I know this sounds crazy, and I'm kind of embarrassed about it, but I think I'm supposed to pray for you two. Do you mind?"

We said we needed all the prayer we could get. She got out of her chair, and before we could move, she knelt in front of us, wrapped her arms around us, and started to pray, her South African–accented words rich in reverence, gentle in spirit, insistent with God. Before the end of her first sentence, my eyes had moistened; by her last, I had given way to a shoulder-shaking, tear-flowing, snot-running cry.

Tom and Martha are there on the beach now, along with John and Diane, and Jim and Matilda—new friends who have offered me constant kindness and support. Which brings me to Matilda. For many years, she has been my wife's closest friend, a true kindred spirit. I have married into this relationship, as it were, and now it's hard to imagine life without her laughter, her mock-Irish accent, her passionate spirituality. Whenever I see her I want to cause a scene by hugging her for a very long time. I want her to know how much I love her. She is slightly crazy, as are most of the saints, I suppose. If the Apostle said, "Bear one another's burdens, and in this way you will fulfill the law of Christ,"[3] she is just foolish enough to believe these words and take them as a literal possibility. So when she knows I'm going through a particularly difficult time, she asks God for my pain and sorrow, and this is the truth: God grants her request so fully she is not able to get out of bed, so weakened is she by the suffering.

There is a community around me, oh yes, and we're making our way along the water's edge. Now, though, I realize we have to look down to see sand and water. We are not walking but flying. I'm in the middle of an airborne squadron of compassion. For many years I was in the lead, working hard to stay up front, but now they've let me fall back and they're breaking the wind for me and flapping their wings extra hard to create the turbulence I need to stay aloft.

This flock of support that surrounds me is also the Church. I cannot let myself forget this. It has no organizational structure, no committees (thank God!), and no set liturgies. But if I understand my New Testament, the community helping me fly is more faithful to the real work of the Church than the denomination now trying to figure out what to do with me. Theologians will warn me about a false distinction between the Church as an institution and the Church as a fellowship; to separate them, they will remind me, leads to a disembodied Christianity. They may be right. Perhaps it's best to see both as part of one indivisible community, at once sinful and holy, or to use Luther's image, a streetwalker and the Bride of Christ. All I can tell you is that one group has tried to cut my wings and another group has helped me get off the ground.

The institution, as an embodied, earthly reality, shaped by psychological and sociological forces, has had to punish me. This punishment may well serve necessary institutional needs; I should have expected everything meted out to me. But it has also worked against my healing and restoration. How could it have done other? It was based on condemnation, and condemnation does not lead toward redemption. John's Gospel tells us that "God did not send the Son into the world to condemn the world, but in order that the world might be saved through him."[4] Condemnation and salvation are at eternal cross-purposes.

The "discipline" that was supposed to . . . what? . . . help me see the error of my ways, I guess, and make me repentant and reform me, has really had the opposite effect. It has made me defensive. Those who have wanted to ensure my remorse have actually hardened me. This may be one reason Jesus condemned a judgmental spirit. It doesn't work. If you pound a person who has failed, there will be at least a small part of him that knows he isn't *all* bad, and that part will rise up to protect itself. The Ken Starrs of this world may serve useful purposes, but whatever good they do, they will never turn Bill Clintons into better men. When I first confessed my sin to my wife and a few friends, I was overcome by sorrow. My guilt was global, contaminating everything in my life. But as my failure became more public, and as the Church tried to force an official, institutionally certified repentance on me, the anger that had been turned inward was redirected outward; it was as though something within me had to circle the wagons and keep dodging flaming arrows—and that left little time for personal introspection. I had to fight to stay alive.

On the other hand, the grace I have received from those who have loved me has truly humbled me. No one has condoned my sin. No one has been anything but saddened by my actions. But all have stayed committed to me. They affirmed me when I despised myself, and they believed in me when I doubted myself. They have been my Babemba tribe, encircling me with reminders of the good in my life. Most of all, they have forgiven me, and their forgiveness has brought me to my knees in repentance, their embrace has filled me with desire to be a better man, their loyalty has made me want to be worthy of them. A line from "Amazing Grace" gets it just right: " 'Twas grace that taught my heart to fear and grace my fears relieved." Grace is the only judgment that can redeem. Unmerited mercy is the only power that can save.

9

HELD ALOFT

Grace. No word better describes the flight of brown pelicans. Clumsy on ground and gawky in takeoff, but once airborne an epiphany. Their soaring manifests a near-perfect conjunction of elemental forces: form and function and freedom come together in a conspiracy of loveliness to overturn all notions of avian flight.

Stand with me on this wintry beach. A February wind bites our faces; we will want to pocket our hands as we wait. Before long, though, we will see them coming. A line will glide overhead, with four or perhaps forty, and what you will notice first, I promise, is stillness. Each bird will slip motionless through the air. No frantic flapping. No noisy squawking. You will see only the occasional movement of wings, one downward stroke, maybe two, executed with nonchalance, almost indifference, and then only silent soaring, effortless elegance.

If cormorants happen to pass, our eyes will not avoid the frantic exertion. The poor critters will beat the air with hysterical energy, never daring to pause. Air is an enemy, a foe to be vanquished. We will be out of breath just watching, and a little embarrassed. Turning back to the pelicans will be like turning to Mikhail Baryshnikov after watching me dance; the relief and delight will be impossible to overstate.

You will wonder how far they can glide without flapping

wings. My eyes have followed them for the answer, and they have passed overhead and completely out of sight without my observing even a single twitch of a wing. They do not fight the air; they ride it, become one with it. They bring to mind Isadora Duncan's comment: "Some dancers dance to the music. I dance the music." Some birds fly in the air. Pelicans fly the air.

Forty million years of survival on the margins have taught them how to do this. Perhaps it did not come easily; perhaps their ancestors evolved through stages of furious flapping. But they have now mastered the mysteries: they mount wind that blows across the face of the deep; they ride invisible currents that rise heavenward; they rest on creation's invisible breath. Flying for pelicans means allowing themselves to be held aloft. They ascend thermals, the warmer columns of air, to great heights. When these are absent or headwinds are a problem, they descend almost to sea level, and with wings nearly touching water they practice the technique of "troughing"—gliding through the valleys between waves and resting on the cushion of air that rises up from the water beneath them. It's a sight to make youngsters giggle and oldsters thank God they're still alive to behold it.

Here at the beach, watching these pelicans, a conviction slowly forms within me, a vague awareness grows into firm certainty: the only way to fly is to rest on the breath blowing up from the face of the Deep. For many years I have worked like a cormorant, fearful that any pause would lead to a crash. The hard labor, in retrospect, was unnecessary, but I was too busy to see it at the time, too busy with important endeavors to notice that it was, in part, really a struggle—a contending with others, with myself, and even with God. Now, perhaps because of weariness or because I have no idea what else to do, I'm ready to allow an unseen force to support me.

I have always believed it would support me. At the center of my faith has been a conviction that God is *for* the world in general and me in particular, and that the essential New Testament message is "God is love."[1] A God like this can be counted on to lift and carry me, albeit in unseen ways, through the days of my life.

I have often recalled a sermon preached by Paul Tillich in which he speaks of grace striking us like a wave of light breaking into our darkness and "a voice . . . saying: 'You are accepted. *You are accepted,* accepted by that which is greater than you, and the name of which you do not know. Do not ask for the name now; perhaps you will find it later. Do not try to do anything now; perhaps later you will do much. Do not seek for anything; do not perform anything; do not intend anything. *Simply accept the fact that you are accepted!*' If that happens to us, we experience grace. After such an experience we may not be better than before, and we may not believe more than before. But everything is transformed. In that moment, grace conquers sin, and reconciliation bridges the gulf of estrangement. And nothing is demanded of this experience, no religious or moral or intellectual presupposition, nothing but *acceptance.*"[2] To me, these words have always expressed the essential kernel of religious faith.

But it's one thing to know something in the head and another to know it in the guts; it's one thing to be aware of something intellectually and another to engage your whole being with it. The latter sort of knowing, like the Bible's euphemism for sexual intercourse, is an intimate union. It is, I think, the object of our deepest longing, the goal of our fiercest struggles, the fulfillment toward which all eros reaches. But sooner or later we must discover it cannot be grasped, only received. It is the opposite of work. It happens when we cease the feverish beating of wings and surrender to the divine currents that lift and carry us.

. . . . .

About six years ago the light of God went into total eclipse for me, or so it seemed. I was crawling into dark corners of my being. I had no idea where I was going or whether I would survive. But I couldn't go back; the time had come to face problems, some unconscious, I had long avoided. My psychiatrist, Dr. O., was smart enough not to make me feel better, through pills or easy advice, and tough enough to force me to stay in my pain until I found a way into deeper healing. I didn't much like her. She was maddeningly nondirective, given to long periods of silence, and she seemed perfectly content to let me writhe in the pit.

I arrived at her office one day as low as a human being can get. I knew the routine, so I launched into my soliloquy: "I feel terrible. I'm fully, completely, totally depressed."

She said nothing. She wanted me to keep talking, I knew, so I obliged. "I'm really low, as I said, and tired . . . really tired. Weary of everything."

She said nothing.

This time I waited. She wanted silence, I would give her silence. I sat staring at my knees. After a few minutes I gave in and looked up. My eyes begged her to speak to me.

She said, "What's underneath that?"

"Well, loneliness, I guess, and guilt. That's all."

Again, long silence. Then she said, "What's underneath that?"

"I just told you everything. Does it sound like I'm hiding anything? I feel awful and that's all."

"What's underneath that?"

"Well, to be honest, now there is anger. I'm wondering what kind of game you're playing."

"What's underneath that?"

"THERE IS NOTHING UNDERNEATH THAT! AREN'T YOU LISTENING? I'M FEELING SHITTY AND THERE IS NOTHING, NOTHING AT ALL UNDER THAT!"

"Nothing?" she asked quietly.

Tears started streaming down my cheeks, followed by rivers. It was as though the ground opened beneath me, or Atlantis rose up out of the sea, or heaven crashed into earth. All reality changed in that instant. I had fallen, all the way down, into the depths of my hell, and I discovered that underneath was not nothing but something—a something that was really Someone, Someone who was not impressed with my failures, Someone who had never rejected me, Someone who had accepted me before the beginning of time, Someone who was holding me and would never, never let me go.

"No," I finally choked out. "There is . . . God."

And then she did something I will never forget, something that said more than all the previous hours of therapy combined: she nodded.

It was as though all her silence and indirection had been the result of careful pruning, all for the purpose of leaving the one wondrous rose of that nod. She was saying everything I needed to hear: "Now you know, Dr. Big Shot Seminary President, you who preach and teach and write about grace, *now you know.*"

Now I know. Unfortunately, I don't always remember what I know. Events of the past year—the trial and public humiliation and gulls crapping on my head—have often distracted me and kept me from grasping this important reality. Perhaps it doesn't matter. Grace, after all, is not about *me* grasping anything; grace means that I have already been grasped, and by a love that will not let me go.

In this season of living at the margins, God has been as mysterious as the ocean lapping at my feet. Old certainties have disappeared like sand during winter tides, leaving rocks painful to

walk over. But everything seems to be sifting down to one fundamental choice: either God is not a God of grace, or God is indeed
gracious beyond our human understanding.

If God is *not* a God of grace, if Jesus did not reveal the character of God, if I have been wrong all these years, the Church's exclusion of me and the condemnation I have received from
individuals *simply doesn't matter.* Worrying about these things
would be like whining at not being invited to dine with the captain of the *Titanic.* I would have far larger and finally insur-
mountable reasons for despair.

On the other hand, if grace *is* the central truth about God, this
is a Mystery I want to stay near. Living along its edge may still be
confusing, and I may often stumble around in the fog of doubt,
but again this must be said: *it doesn't matter.* For if the Mystery is
benign and life-giving and eternally loving, then I do not need to
comprehend its hidden currents. The wind blowing off it can
keep me aloft. What have I to lose? If I fall, I fall into the Deep, I
fall into a place no more dangerous than the Everlasting Arms. It
will be no *less* dangerous, of course; the Deep is never safe. But its
danger exists within a grand adventure, its pain is part of a pro-
founder joy, its judgment serves a final salvation.

When the choice is put this starkly, I can do nothing other
than to keep believing in a God who relates to the world—including me—with grace, a God who, in the man Jesus, entered
fully into our humanity, its joys and sorrows, to redeem it from
within and lead it toward a goal that will be the fulfillment of our
deepest longings, a goal the Bible describes in images such as
"kingdom" or "resurrection" or "heaven." This God, moreover,
continues to blow the divine Spirit across the unformed, threatening darkness of our lives to bring creation out of chaos, life out
of death. On this breath I can rest; with the lift of this wind I can
soar.

Perhaps I have simply fallen back on a familiar paradigm, the structure of reality in which I have lived my whole life. But what advantage is there in the alternative? It must surely lead to absolute despair. More important, there is this: what I saw at the bottom of the pit. It was not nothing but something; it was Someone with a will to save, Someone who was holding me.

Grace invites a retrospective look over the shoulder. My past did not happen apart from its guiding influence. To make this statement, in a sense, transforms everything. Even my failures, in the light of grace, are shown to be less than my guilt has made them. They are no longer absolute. Perhaps I should think of them in quotation marks—"failures"—because they have been stripped of their dignity. There is an essential falseness to them. I am not simply saying that human motives are complex, that my infidelity, to name one wrongdoing, happened in tandem with love, that even that which was bad was also good. This is true, so far as it goes. I'm saying something more important: my "failure" has an inferior status next to God's determination to work through it; my sin, however egregious, has a borrowed reality, because ultimately it will be used *by God's grace* for good and even holy purposes. "Where sin increased," St. Paul said, "grace abounded all the more."[3] According to Christian faith, God has used the crucifixion of Jesus, the worst "acting out" of human disobedience, for the redemption of the world. Dare I imagine that my screw-ups are too much for God, beyond the pale of hope? There is no need to add absurdity to my list of "failures."

Then comes the next step, difficult to take. What is true for me must also be true for others: their "failures," too, can serve the purposes of grace. The Church "discipline" that has pounded me, the judgmental individuals who have condemned me, the public humiliation, and the uncertainty of my future—the whole damn mess can be turned into a blessed mess, the things that have beaten the hell out of me can be used to beat heaven into me. St. Augustine once prayed, "And you, O Lord, stood in the secret places of my soul, by a severe mercy redoubling my lashes of fear and shame, lest I should give way again."[4] God's mercy has a severe side to it; grace flows from a Mystery that is often storm-tossed and very threatening. But I have to believe—I *have to* believe—that God has been working for good purposes through it all.

A line of pelicans soaring above me glides along unseen currents, clearly at peace with themselves and their world. I think of lines from Gerard Manley Hopkins: "My heart in hiding / Stirred for a bird,—the achieve of, the mastery of the thing!"[5]

My wonder increases as I realize I am flying with them. I, too, have a certain mastery of the thing! There is no pride in this. I am more mastered than mastering. Flying is not my own doing, I know. Grace has drawn me to this marginal place, and grace has awakened a longing for flight, and grace has been at work in my halfhearted rituals of preparation, and grace has surrounded me with fellow pelicans, and grace now lifts and steadies me and whispers promises of a future. I can even imagine the courage to dive deeply into the Mystery below. I do not have it yet, but I can at least imagine it, anticipate its arrival. Flying is emboldening me, destroying my fear. I am soaring, held aloft, by a force I can trust. Grace.

10

SILENCE

*A*lthough I have observed pelicans for years and studied them for months, I have never been aware of their silence—until I read, "As they mature, brown pelicans lose their vocal powers and become almost mute. For this reason, the drama of colonization, flight, and the spectacular ritual of diving for food is a silent one."[1] It occurred to me that I had never actually *heard* a pelican. Can you *ever* hear them? I'm listening closely to find out. I'm almost daring them to squeak or squawk or sound off in some way; I'm as attentive as a mother listening for the door after her teenager's curfew. I've heard nothing. Except the silence, and that's something, really, something that can be quite loud once it speaks.

The only time you hear pelicans is when they're chicks. Like all youngsters, they create a ruckus, peeping and screaming and carrying on. But as they mature, they become quiet.

Does this silence have anything to do with their survival at the margins?

Walker Percy, in his novel *The Second Coming,* poses the question, "Is it possible for people to miss their lives in the same way one misses a plane?" Percy describes such a life: "Not once in his entire life has he allowed himself to come to rest in the quiet center of himself but had forever cast himself forward from some dark past he could not remember to a future that did not exist. Not once had he been present for his life. So his life had passed like a dream."[2]

These past few years I have been casting myself between a dark past and a nonexistent future, and instead of getting anywhere worthwhile I have nearly missed the plane. Too hard at work, I have not rested in the quiet center of myself. I have been busy telling my side of the story, setting the record straight. I have ignored Will Durant's comment that "one of the lessons of history is that nothing is often a good thing to do and always a clever thing to say."[3] I had the sense to muzzle my mouth when the story broke to the public at large; as reporters telephoned and tried to ambush me, I knew anything beyond a brief statement would entangle me in a mess of misquotation and misstatements that would make matters worse. Once my failure was no longer news, however, I was eager to speak to anyone who would listen. The English language would be my sword, and I would charge the enemy, dismembering rumors and half-truths and malicious lies, and I would win a victory for truth. Also a victory for me. I told myself this was beside the point; secretly, though, I knew it was very much to the point. If you feel maligned, self-justification is an instinctive response.

Moreover, truth is a complicated matter. It includes facts, and also motives and context and meanings. For example, a man may have taken a car that didn't belong to him, but it makes a difference whether he stole it for a drunken joyride or borrowed it to speed a dying man to the hospital. Truth calls for more than any one person knows; in some ways, it's a community project. I have simply wanted to be involved. Although I can offer nothing to lift my story onto high moral ground, I have wanted to contribute my two cents' worth.

Never mind that two cents isn't worth much. A wrecking ball has smashed my world, and much that I have loved is now rubble. I have wanted to clean up the mess and rebuild, so I have reached for my favorite tool—language. I have been what Malcolm Muggeridge called a "vendor of words," speaking and writing my way to professional success. With words I have built an identity, and naturally, now that it has fallen to pieces I have again reached for them to repair it.

A significant part of anyone's identity is relationships with others. Our sense of self is shaped, in large measure, through interaction with family, friends, colleagues, and God; by these relationships we gain self-awareness and find a place in the world. I need to reconstruct these, and words have seemed the best—even necessary—way to do this. I have spoken, therefore, not solely for self-justification, but to enable understanding and forgiveness and reconciliation.

Behind all this is the conviction that words *do* something. Words work. As evident in the last few paragraphs, active verbs have crowded my thoughts: *explain, build, reconstruct, repair, reconcile*—words that labor and sweat. I have wanted to fix things, so I have spat in my palms and reached for my preferred tool and swung for all I'm worth.

Why? I have to ask myself this question.

If grace is indeed the force that lifts and carries me toward my destiny as a creature of flight, it is both foolish and wasteful to trust my own furious flapping. The New Testament sets a choice before us: we are saved either by grace or by works. One or the other. If God works on my behalf, dare I take matters into my own hands, laboring with wrinkled-browed intensity and set-jawed determination to make things conform to my will?

Grace inevitably leads to primal silence. Mercy strikes us mute with wonder and trust. Words have an appropriate place, to be sure, especially those of gratitude and witness, but they come later. First, silence: the silence of reverence before God's good work, the silence of rest from *doing,* the silence of simple *being.* This is why masters of spirituality have always commended silence. "Silence is the royal road to spiritual formation," wrote Henri Nouwen. Perhaps it is the only road. The word of grace must quiet all words of self-justification and explanation and control.

Almost everything in our culture works against this silence. The information explosion has created a deafening blast, and it is nearly impossible to escape the noise. Ten years ago it was estimated that the average American was exposed to fifteen hundred commercial messages every day. One can only imagine what that number is a decade later, now that the Internet connects with every home and office, and cell phones ring in every purse and pocket. The average office worker is bombarded by just under two hundred telephone, e-mail, voice mail, postal, and other communications every day—and studies show that many struggle to cope. They are also, oddly, eager for more, afraid to miss a single message: carrying pagers, logging in to e-mail, adding "call waiting" to telephones, watching television six hours a day.

Sensory stimulation is addictive. To deliver the same jolt, nerves must be hit harder and harder. *American Bandstand* becomes MTV and the NFL becomes the XFL. The din gets louder and louder.

And there may be another reason for the noise. We may be afraid of what the silence says. As I pastor I sometimes led my congregation in prayers of silence. I soon learned to use my watch because I couldn't trust my sense of time with only silence between me and eight hundred others. I would judge the quiet to have lasted many minutes, when really it had been only seconds.

The quiet seemed to draw us into a space in which time, through mysterious laws of relativity, had been stretched beyond anything we had known. As seconds ticked away, the fidgeting I felt within myself and the restlessness I heard in the congregation (coughs, whispering, movement in the pews) came from somewhere deep within each of us, a place of fear. What if we actually heard God—*God!*—speak? This would be too upsetting, too disruptive, not the nice comfortable religion we had counted on to provide a little peace and comfort. Worse, what if, as our doubts had warned, we didn't hear anything? What if there was *only* the silence? What if God didn't show up as promised?

Silence threatens to tell us more than we want to know. If we stop the chatter long enough to listen, we may hear only nothing—a nothing that would speak an unbearable terror, a nothing that would be a resounding, "See! Your worst fears are true. You *are* alone in a quiet, cold universe." Silence might be a doorway into a more threatening, cosmic emptiness.

Despite my faith in a good and gracious God, this fear has probably been underneath all my talking and writing and internal debates. But I have come to the beach to escape the distracting cacophony both around me and within me; I have come to listen to the insistent waves of Mystery breaking onto the sands of my heart.

I am standing on the bluff of a cliff rising about fifty feet above the beach. In the distance, a ragged V-formation is flying toward me. They are getting closer and closer, and they glide along air currents, scarcely a wing moving, to within a few feet of me. If I stretch out my hand, I might be able to touch them. I see a ribbon of white feathers along their heads and necks; I notice the red tint on the tip of their bills.

"Good afternoon," I say, "and . . . thanks." I'm not sure what to say, but I feel I should communicate in some way, and as usual, I rely on words. They make no sound, soaring with silence so absolute it seems an echo of the primeval Nothing. Suddenly something within me jerks awake, jumps as though startled by a loud voice. Maybe I'm losing touch with reality. This is what I hear: *relax, trust the currents, be at peace.* Their quietness has an authority I wouldn't dare question.

As soon as they pass, the formation breaks. Several stop midflight, as though suspended by invisible wires, almost hovering like helicopters. They've probably spotted a school of fish. In an instant they upend themselves and dive into the sea, bobbing to the surface a few seconds later with bulging pouches. And through it all, they remain silent.

Pelicans are the most gregarious of birds: they do everything together, as I have said, yet they utter no sounds. Clearly they have learned to communicate despite silence, or perhaps through silence.

Silence is most often understood in negative terms. It is *not* something: not speech, not imparting information, not "vibrations transmitted through . . . solid, liquid, or gas, with frequencies in the approximate range of 20 to 20,000 hertz, capable of being detected by human organs of hearing"[4] (as my dictionary defines "sound"). Silence is absence, we think, emptiness.

Though it may well be an aural void, it is surely not a communication void. Silence can convey a great deal, if we know how to listen. When Ralph Waldo Emerson visited Europe, he called on Thomas Carlyle. The notoriously reticent host gave Emerson a pipe, as he took one for himself. They sat smoking until bedtime—in complete silence. On parting they shook hands cordially, congratulating each other on the fruitful time they had enjoyed together.[5]

For me, sitting in silence is not always fruitful. Sometimes quietness emboldens demons and agitates my imagination to new aggressiveness. I do not blame the silence for this; my want of discipline is at fault, I'm sure. Often, though, silence does bestow gifts—gifts I cannot grasp, only receive. This is why I keep trying it, often in the dark of early morning with a warm coffee mug, or at the water's edge, sitting on the sand or running along the beach. Sometimes, in these moments, I hear whispered intimations of good news. I cannot summon them; they arrive, like wind across water, from a force beyond my control. Most often, they remind me of what I've heard before, in the aftermath of brokenness, in complete exhaustion, in the resignation of nothing left to say. They tell me once more that underneath it all—down below the layers of doubt and depression—there is Someone with arms outstretched, Someone holding me, Someone who can be trusted.

In his poem "Ash Wednesday," T. S. Eliot wrote, "And pray to God to have mercy upon us / And I pray that I may forget / These matters that with myself I too much discuss / Too much explain. . . ."[6] In silence comes the granting of this request, the beginning of merciful forgetting. I even begin to feel able to relinquish self-justification and my desire to set the record straight. I know that even if no one else understands, God does, and that is enough.

Henry Ward Beecher, the most famous preacher of the 1870s and pastor of Brooklyn's Plymouth Church, was accused of "criminal conversation" with Elizabeth Tilton, the wife of his longtime friend Theodore. The six-month trial was for its day what the O. J. Simpson trial was for ours. It captivated national attention and ended inconclusively. Did they actually commit adultery?

Opinions divided, with intense convictions on both sides. Uncertainty was magnified because during the trial Elizabeth denied wrongdoing, yet four years later changed her story and confessed to an intimate relationship. Criticized by newspapers as a weak, vacillating woman who could not be trusted, she said she would "leave the truth with God." Historian Richard Wightman Fox, in a recent book exploring the scandal, suggests that "maybe she meant only that God would know she was telling the truth, and his opinion was all that mattered to her. But maybe she wished her phrase to mean that the truth in this instance was of a magnitude and complexity that only God *could* understand. Only his perspective was large enough, dispassionate and magnanimous enough, to encompass all the wrinkles of all the stories—stories more or less true, stories partially true, stories with slivers of truth in them—that had been and were being told about herself and the two men she loved."[7]

What silence grants is Sabbath rest from the work of words. This gift is not easily received by a man whose self-worth has been intimately connected with achievements and professional recognition. Without these things he has done, who is he? He has always been a preacher and counselor and leader and doer of good works. Now that he is none of these things, who is he? When he meets people, they say, "What do you do?" which of course means, "Who are you?" and he has no idea what to say. He wants to say "beach bum" but he thinks they won't understand, and having people understand has always been important to him. So he keeps quiet, mostly, and out of that silence, out of that nothing-left-to-say-or-do, out of that Sabbath rest, a conviction is growing. He is not, and never has been, what he *does;* he is only, and always has been, who he *is*. And this is who he is: a man beloved by God, saved by grace. At every point, it seems, he is inexorably pressed to accept this acceptance, to affirm this affirmation.

What the ancient prophet said to people busily strategizing for self-defense must be true: "In returning and rest you shall be saved; in quietness and trust shall be your strength."[8]

11

FORCES

BEYOND CONTROL

*S*ometimes, when I'm trying to be silent, I hear myself asking, "Why? Why did I earn a Ph.D. in Jackassology?" That's easy to answer: I used my freedom as God's child to break God's laws. But after repentance and trying to make amends and years of counseling, why was I so harshly condemned? Why did I lose my job? Why did my life have to unravel so completely? Why hasn't God stepped in a little sooner to set things right?

Important questions sooner or later get down to God. *Why do bad things happen?* leads inevitably to *Why does God allow bad things to happen?* Those who have attempted to answer this question have provoked considerable disagreement. Some see God causing all things to happen, like a puppeteer pulling all strings. Some see God providing overall direction, like an orchestra conductor. Some see God working toward a good goal, like a weaver blending light and dark threads into a work of art. Some see God granting human freedom and waiting to see what will happen, like a Little League coach letting the kids play on their own. Each explanation offered has strengths and weaknesses, each answers questions but raises others, and each struggles to hold together elements that, from a human perspective, mix as well as oil and water: God's sovereignty and human freedom, God's love and human suffering. And each, I'm sorry to say, leaves unanswered the question *Why?*

I am observing my disciplines of preparation, mostly. I spend the first hour of every day in prayer and meditation. I attend Sunday worship. I have not yet offered significant service to others, I'm sorry to report, except to be attentive to the needs of my family and friends, which I suppose is the first and most important step toward a charitable life; I had hoped by now, though, to be volunteering in a food bank or teaching English to migrant workers or delivering clothes to the Navajo reservation. But that hope has been motivated, I suppose, more by a stubborn desire for self-redemption than by gratitude for God's grace.

And I am still running. Every other day, about seven miles. Most of the time it feels good, though I have recently been slowed by plantar fasciitis, doctor-talk for something like a nail puncturing my heel. I'm told it happens to fifty-one-year-old runners. Serious athletes have the guts to endure it, even welcome it as proof of transcending courage and commitment. I grumble about it, asking God why middle age has to be so difficult. But I keep kicking out the distance, going to the beach at low tide, when there is plenty of level, hard sand.

Today I'm running through a gray world. All horizons have disappeared in a monochromatic singularity of sea and sky and soul. Everything around me seems marred by loss, broken in some way. As usual, I'm watching for sand dollars, the nearly circular echinoderms with the delicate etching of five palm fronds. I have decided to see them as a sign of God's blessing, perhaps because they are fragile and easily overlooked. On a good day I find two or three; once I came home with six in perfect condition. This afternoon I have seen nothing but crushed ones, stepped on by a careless force.

Winter tides have washed away much of the sand. For about a quarter of a mile, it has fully disappeared, leaving nothing but hard rocks to torture my already sore feet. I'm looking for an alternate route, perhaps one along the sandstone cliffs; the cliffs, though, have been devoured by voracious waves at high tide and erosion makes them unsafe.

A man and woman wave me down, obviously needing assistance. Their accents suggest Australian tourists. They found a small seal, far from water's edge and apparently sick. "What should we do?" they ask. I have no idea what to do, but it feels good to be treated, once again, as an authority, a problem solver, a leader in a situation of crisis. So I approach the seal, bending over him, as though I were actually making a knowledgeable diagnosis.

"He's sick," I said.

They keep looking at me, wanting something a little more helpful. I try to oblige. Having taken up the mantle of authority, it's not easy to set it down. "We should call Animal Control," I say. "They'll probably send someone right over." By "we" I meant "you," because I was wearing only shorts and a sweatshirt, and obviously I had no way to make a call. We wait only about fifteen seconds before someone walks past holding a cell phone to her ear. She is eager to help, so I decide it wouldn't appear insensitive to continue my run.

As I head down the beach, I wonder what will become of the seal. He will probably die. I recall the last time I had been running and needed money for a call. I was on the cliffs above Del Mar Beach, along the railroad tracks. I saw a woman sitting in the middle of the tracks. That was dangerous, I thought, but didn't pay much attention. Until I heard an approaching train. She didn't move, and I started running faster, and the sound of the train got louder and louder, and still she didn't move, and I ran faster still. It wasn't heroism but sheer instinct that made me lunge at her. I dragged her off the tracks just as the train came roaring by us. I can still feel the *shwoosh* of the train speeding past, my heart pounding, and her quivering shoulders under my arm. "Why did you save me? Why did you save me?" she whimpered. At the time, I didn't understand how pain could be so grievous, how despair could be so total, that she would want to die. Later, under the accumulated weight of my life, I would think of her with greater sympathy.

Whatever became of her? Did she pass through her dark night and wake to a better day? Or did forces arrayed against her seem so overwhelming that, on another day, she lay on tracks until a heedless locomotive brought release?

The depression I'm feeling is making it difficult for the endorphins to work their magic. My spirit is a crushed sand dollar, my faith an eroded cliff, my optimism a sick seal. Everywhere I see gray. I'm ready to turn around and head home.

Then I see, at some distance, a lone bird flying. The set of its wings and the ease of its flight tell me it's a pelican. I keep running toward him, as he flies toward me. As he nears, I stop. "It must be nice to soar above it all," I say to him, and in my words I hear weariness and anger and even some accusation. It's stupid, I know. He's just a bird; he shares no responsibility for the brokenness of this world and my life. But there he is, soaring with such . . . peace.

He is now so close I can see red—the tip of his bill, the rim of his eye. I wonder what that eye has seen, how things appear from his vantage point. Does he notice a dying seal? Or have millions of years of evolution bestowed a merciful selective perception, trained his sight for simple survival? And for some reason—in the way one thought leads to another, in a stream of consciousness that meanders through strange twists and turns—I remember and start singing the old spiritual, "Nobody knows the troubles I've seen. ...."

In the pelican's case, it's not the troubles he's seen but the ones he hasn't that have caused grief. Buckshot from hunters, invisible fishing lines, chemicals—all from humans, who came near destroying a creature whose species has survived for forty million years.

At the turn of the twentieth century, pelican hunting was a big and bloody business in the state of Florida; it was not meat that attracted hunters but feathers. The extermination might have claimed every bird, had not a warden from the National Audubon Society, gathering evidence of the hunting, been killed. Floridians were suddenly outraged and demanded that Washington do something about a situation that had gotten out of control. President Theodore Roosevelt, an ardent environmentalist, issued an executive order in 1903 setting aside Pelican Island as the first in a network of national wildlife refuges (the system has grown to more than three hundred sanctuaries around the country).

Brown pelicans are the state bird of Louisiana, where they resided in abundance—until the middle of the last century, when they started dying off in large numbers. No analyses of eggs or tissue were conducted, so biologists remain uncertain about the exact cause. Very likely, however, chemicals were to blame. From 1943 to 1963 agricultural pesticides were used with increasing frequency in the Mississippi Delta. Cotton, the area's major crop, is particularly vulnerable to damage from insects. So through the summer months aerial bombardments released millions of pounds of DDT, endrin, and other compounds, many toxic to warm-blooded animals. Other factors, such as severe weather, also may have contributed, but whatever the reasons, an entire population was destroyed. In the late sixties scientists began a reintroduction program that has been largely successful, and today hundreds of the birds can be seen.

Pelicans in California prefer to nest on islands, their favorites being the Coronado Islands of Mexico seventeen miles south of San Diego, and the Channel Islands west of Santa Barbara, especially Anacapa, a rocky four-mile-long remnant of a mountain peak nine miles from the coastline. For years, Anacapa was the preferred nesting ground for West Coast pelicans.

In March 1969, a group of biologists, led by Dr. Robert Risebrough of the University of California, visited Anacapa. They found approximately three hundred pairs of birds nesting on the western end of the island, and all seemed in order. Closer examination, however, revealed something startling: the nests were empty, or the few eggs that lay there were crushed. Dr. Risebrough returned in mid-April to discover a deserted colony; all the parent pelicans had vanished. Extensive analysis of egg remains blamed the chemical DDT.

I first heard about DDT in college. This was one of the things we protested in those days, thanks to the emerging environmentalist movement. I thought of it as pure poison, evidence of raw corporate greed. But it's important to recall the compound's history. Originally discovered in an English laboratory in 1874, it proved a major boon to agriculture. It was first used as a moth-proofing agent, and later in the fight against insect-borne disease. It has been estimated that it was directly responsible for saving a hundred million human lives. There are at least two sides to most stories, which makes life maddeningly ambiguous. Something intended for good purposes can, down the line, have deadly consequences.

By the mid-fifties DDT was hailed as an effective weapon against agricultural pests. It was applied liberally to the land, eventually finding its way to the sea, where it accumulated in surface plankton and became part of the food chain. The plankton was eaten by fish, and the fish were eaten by pelicans. At each level, the chemical was not merely passed on but intensified through what scientists call *biological magnification,* which refers to the accumulation of a chemical in fatty tissues and its increasing toxicity as it travels up the chain. By the time it reached pelicans, DDT was strong enough to cause the thinning of eggshells, which were then crushed under the weight of incubating parents. As a result, pelicans in California were seriously endangered. When DDT was banned in 1972, the population began a dramatic comeback. On one of the Coronado Islands, for example, not a single pelican fledged in 1969, but by 1974 the number had skyrocketed to twelve hundred.[1]

Oh yes, the pelican flying overhead could easily sing, "Nobody knows the troubles I've seen. . . ." Or at least the troubles his kin have seen. I haven't even mentioned commercial fisherman who intentionally destroy them, idiotic motorboaters who use them as target practice, and monsters who cut off their mandibles. Many troubles, many troubles. The pelican could ask *Why?* and maybe does, for all I know. But I suspect that question has lost its urgency through the millennia; the challenges of coping may well have tutored the species toward a wisdom that confesses an unavoidable truth: to be part of creation means experiencing forces beyond control—forces that may be questioned and fought, but must always be suffered. Pelicans have not simply suffered, but suffered *through* toward survival.

They have survived. The recognition of this overwhelms me as I watch the pelican above me soar with a silent elegance born of peace. *They have survived.* Through forty million years of natural selection, through the last century's assault by humans, they have endured. They have been part of a complex web of life and death, flying with grace through dark storms, so that now, as though the whole evolutionary process had been working toward this very moment, a pelican floats above me with serenity so apparent I'm tempted to call it joy. For me, this pelican is a kind of sacrament—a physical sign of a spiritual reality—contradicting the death around me, a shaft of light breaking through the gray of this day, and a promise that I, too, will survive.

All of us, humans and pelicans and sand dollars, are part of a tangled web of interconnections. From it we receive the gift of life and the curse of death, and thus also—for humans, at least—pleasure and pain, happiness and sorrow, anxiety and peace. In addition to biological magnification, we must acknowledge a moral and spiritual magnification. The good and evil done by our ancestors have been passed to us, with the result that we now live far from Eden in a land both beautiful and broken. The tangled web is not delicate gossamer but a chain-link fence. We feel entrapped by forces beyond our control. Where is God in all this? Theologians will formulate answers and we may, at times, inch toward a greater understanding. With or without it, though, we must endure, carry on, survive without lying down on the tracks.

To complicate matters further, we each do our part to beautify or break the world. The choices we make affect those around us and following us, and it's not always easy to discern what is good, let alone what is best. East of Eden things are rarely pure. Good can have evil consequences; DDT, which originally granted life, was passed through the food chain until it caused death. And evil can result in good; the death of pelicans, by alerting us to the dangers of DDT, helped protect life. In my own case, I didn't wake up one morning and decide to do something bad; I didn't consciously set out to hurt people. It was first this step, then that, nothing terrible in itself, until before I knew it I was down a road I had never planned to travel. There was honest love as well as dishonest betrayal in what I did, and through a kind of moral magnification, it grew into a snarl involving many others and much unintended hurt. And similarly, the reaction toward me, often intending noble purposes (healing and restoration), was a blending of intermingled motives, so that what was meant to build up actually beat down, what was meant to bestow healing actually dealt judgment.

What does it mean? Where is it all leading? *Why?*

The novelist Reynolds Price said, "The need is . . . for credible news that our lives proceed in order toward a pattern which, if tragic here and now, is ultimately pleasing in the mind of a god who sees a totality and *at last* enacts His will. We crave nothing less than a perfect story; and while we chatter or listen all our lives in a den of craving—jokes, anecdotes, novels, dreams, films, plays, songs, half the words of our days—we are satisfied only by the one short tale we feel to be true."[2]

We want to believe that the mystery of our lives, inscrutable and inexplicable, is part of a Holy Mystery, a Blessed Force that, though beyond our control, moves purposefully toward a goodness we can now only faintly sense in the depths of our longings. We want to believe that we will, by a gracious salvation, somehow survive.

In the past few months I have found few, if any, answers to my questions. God remains as mysterious as ever. Nonetheless, a conviction is growing within me that I will survive. Like the pelican above, I am supported by a strong, uplifting force. It may blow in gales and zephyrs alike, always beyond my control, breathing desperate urgency into the question *Why?*, but it will blow *for me*, in and through the confusions of my life, toward a wholeness I can now only barely imagine and imperfectly desire.

I believe this, not because I see a pelican in flight, but because, like the pelican, I am part of a larger story. At the center of this story is an act of self-giving love, a surprising reversal in which what was meant to deal judgment actually bestowed healing.

12

BACK TO ORIGINS

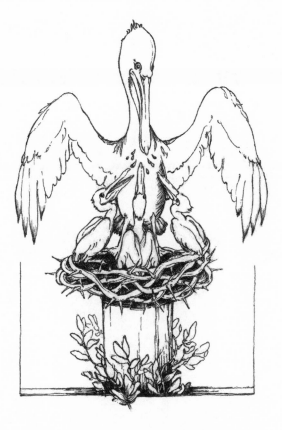

"We are a narrative species," writes Roger Rosenblatt, reflecting on the dying message of Lieutenant Captain Dimitri Kolesnikov to his wife, which had been recovered from the sunken Russian submarine *Kursk*. "We exist by storytelling—by relating our situations—and the test of our evolution may lie in getting the story right."[1]

Stories supply a necessary framework for understanding one's self and world. Some are small ("I discovered we had no milk and went to the market to buy more"), and some are large ("We hold these truths to be self-evident, that all men are created equal, that they are endowed by their Creator with certain unalienable Rights"). The larger ones are sometimes called metanarratives or myths. They exert a powerful influence over us. A skinhead in the Aryan Nations lives by a particular myth, and a priest serving in a city slum lives by another. Stories always *mean* something; this meaning shapes the course of our lives.

I have had to edit my experiences, as we all must, on the way toward finding an understandable narrative. I stand by it as "true," recognizing others will have their own stories. To be saved from the narrowness of my own perspective, it's vitally important that mine becomes part of a larger narrative that provides a deeper and broader meaning.

. . . .

On the day William's mother turned her back on him, forcing him out of the nest and into the world on his own, he fell in with a flotilla of grouchy coots. Their bouncing heads kept rhythm with pumping feet. They were black as the bottom of an old nest, with little white bills used chiefly, it seemed, for jabbing each other.

All at once their heads ducked underwater, leaving William surrounded by black feather-butts. The first to bob up had a silver tail in its beak. So did the second. The third came up with nothing and immediately went down again.

With a bill longer than a whole coot, William thought he might be able to catch something, too. So he plunged his head beneath the surface. In the blurry dimness he saw, at some distance, a large form gliding through strands of seaweed. Everything was silent, foreboding. Then a silvery flash caught his eye. A fish was approaching, just the size to gladden a starving pelican, just the size to fill an empty bird. He lunged at the creature, but it was just beyond reach. William stretched his neck and thrust his pouch and kicked his feet. It was no use. The meal swam by, casually, without concern, without so much as a nod in his direction.

As William was coming up for air, something crashed into the water next to him. It was enough to scare the white stuff out of him. He started paddling with terrified energy, daring only a curious glance back. He saw only foam and ripples. He stopped and turned and stared, wondering what had happened. Before he could take two breaths, the water again erupted, and coming up from the depths was another pelican. His pouch was filled and bulging and writhing.

"That's my fish," William said.

The pelican said nothing. A large hole in his pouch spewed seawater out the right side, which he apparently considered a convenience. He floated patiently, waiting for the drainage.

Three gulls appeared, hoping to share the feast. Two hovered over his bill and one actually landed on his head. He seemed unaware of their presence, or at least unconcerned. He didn't move, except for blinking his eyes, until the only thing left in his pouch was the fish. Then he slowly lifted his head and swallowed. A wriggling lump slid down his throat.

"That was mine," William said again, less with anger than with resignation.

"Did I take it from your pouch?" He didn't actually speak, being an old bird, but somehow William heard him.

"I saw it first."

"You couldn't have wanted it much. You didn't dive."

William was embarrassed to admit he didn't know how to dive. So he said nothing. A swell lifted and dropped them. In the distance, gulls were screeching and squabbling.

"Why quarrel?" the pelican asked. "The Mystery has plenty for all."

"Why did you just sit there and let a gull crap on your head?"

"They tend to do that when they're on your head. At other times, too."

"But why did you let him?"

"Gulls do what gulls do."

"But now you have a mess running down the back of your neck."

"The Mystery will wash it away."

He was a weird bird but better company than coots, and William hoped he wouldn't fly away. "What is *the Mystery*?"

The pelican dipped his bill in the water and splashed it toward William. "What do you call this that holds and feeds us?"

"Well . . ."

"Do you know where it ends?"

"No."

"Do you know its depth? Do you know what it contains? Do you know why it supplies our food and lifts us in flight and draws us to itself?"

"No."

The pelican extended his wings, gave four hard flaps, and was off the water. He ascended a ways before circling back. When directly overhead, he upended himself, angled his wings, and dove straight down. William ducked, shielding himself with his wings, convinced the crazy bird was going to end his short life.

He hit the water about a wing's length away, disappearing briefly before surfacing with another catch. When the stream spouting through his hole became a small trickle, he opened his bill as if to say, "Help yourself." William accepted the charity, too hungry not to, and after downing it offered a grateful belch.

"You may call me Baggs."

"I'm William."

They sat in silence for a while, side by side. In the distance waves crashed against rocks and a couple of seals barked and the gulls were still at it. The quietness opened something within William, and he said, "My mother wouldn't feed me. She just turned away."

"She had to commend you to the mercy of the Mystery. But she wanted to feed you. Remember the Story."

"What Story?" William's eyes were blank.

Baggs could scarcely believe William had not heard the Story. Apparently it was now his responsibility and privilege to tell him. "William, I will tell you the Story, if you wish, and more: I will tell you who you are.

"Once upon a time—a time long ago—Our Mother, the Mother of all our mothers and fathers, was caring for a hatching of chicks. She fed them from the bounty of the Mystery, always catching enough to fill her pouch. But one day a great darkness descended on the face of the Deep. Nothing like it had happened before, and nothing like it has happened since. There were no fish. Our Mother dove and dove, throwing herself deep into the Mystery, but the Mystery yielded nothing. It was as though death had entered the Mystery, or perhaps, strange to say, the Mystery had died.

"With no fish, her young soon grew thin, emaciated. They cried and cried, starving for want of a food she could not provide. So Our Mother started pulling feathers from her chest, one by one, and bared a patch of white, quivering skin. And then, with the tip of her bill—I tell you the truth, William—with the tip of her bill she tore her flesh until it oozed red. She kept pecking as the red flowed down her feathers and covered her bill, kept pecking until a pool formed in the bottom of the nest, kept pecking at her flesh until she had uncovered her beating heart.

" 'Eat, dear ones,' she said. 'Eat and live.' Then she fell beside her young."

William could not move. It was too awful, too wonderful, too . . . he didn't know. "Then what?" he asked Baggs. "What did her chicks do?"

"Must you ask? We're here, aren't we? And William, look at the tip of your bill."

William looked, and what he saw was this: a coloring of red, dark at the tip and flowing back in lighter streaks.

I cannot say that pelicans really tell this story, but humans have told it, again and again—in poems and paintings, in statuary and stained glass. It seems to have risen out of our collective unconscious to point to another story, the Story by which many understand themselves and their world and even God. Early Christians adopted the self-sacrificing mother pelican as a sign of Christ's sacrifice. By the Middle Ages paintings of the crucifixion often included a nest atop the cross, with the blood flowing from the pelican's chest paralleling the blood flowing from Christ's side. The image was set on altarpieces, carved into cathedral stonework, and engraved on chalices.[2] A mother pelican succoring her young with her own warm blood, feeding them from her own heart, seemed a perfect visual representation for the self-giving love of God.

The story of God's self-sacrifice has shaped my life. I heard it as a child, studied it with academic rigor as a young man, preached and taught and wrote about it as an adult. It has provided a structure of meaning for me, a way to understand myself and the world around me. I have had doubts, inevitably present with faith, but I have never turned from it. Even during seasons of confusion and despair the story has seemed to me too strange and wonderful not to be true.

It is the story of a Creator who takes upon himself the burden of our humanity, including our failures and suffering and even our death. It is the story of a Creator who, like a mother pelican, sacrifices herself for the beloved, offering herself in nurturing love. It is the story of God judging sin and humans judging God, and the astonishing transformation of this twofold judgment into reconciliation. It is the story with a cross at its center but not at its end: its plot moves toward the upsetting of all things, the Great Reversal in which the dead Jesus was raised from the tomb, and along with him our hope that death be swallowed up by life eternal.

The central theme of this story is divine love at the center of the universe, a love that seeks and sacrifices and saves, a love that

will overcome all obstacles, a love that will finally bring to fulfillment all good.

In his autobiography, *Brother to a Dragonfly,* Will Campbell
tells of his friendship with P. D. East, someone with whom he
had often argued to a standstill about the truth of Christianity.
One day, as they rode together in a car, East said, "Just tell me
what this Jesus cat is all about. I'm not too bright but maybe I can
get the hang of it. . . . If you could tell me what the hell the Christian faith is about maybe I wouldn't make an ass out of myself
when I'm talking about it. Keep it simple. In ten words or less,
what's the Christian message? . . . Let me have it. Ten words."

Campbell thought hard for several minutes, and then said,
"We're all bastards but God loves us anyway."[3]

This story does not answer the troublesome question *Why?* In
many ways, it intensifies the question and deepens the Mystery
of God. Why would a God who has gone to such trouble to save
us allow us to fall into misery? Why does Love Eternal seem so
indifferent to human suffering? This story at once discloses and
perplexes, explains and confuses, reveals and conceals.

But it shows enough. That's what I affirm with my whole
heart. My mind continues to question and debate, and I experience long hours, if not days, of depression. I still get angry, with
myself and others. Sometimes even with God. But in a deep place
of my being, a place that doesn't contradict rational thought but
encompasses it within a larger whole, I believe God loves me and
is mysteriously present in the whole mess of my life. In the end,
that is enough. After the failure and guilt and confession and forgiveness and condemnation and depression and confusion and
loss and sorrow, after all that has happened in and around me, I

can say with renewed certainty what I blubbered out in my psychiatrist's office, that underneath everything is a God who holds me in the arms of grace.

Circumstances of my life have stripped away my identity. It's frightening to be deep into middle age and not know who you are; it's scary to look in a mirror and see a stranger. Though I would not have chosen it, and in some ways still hate it, I now see this laying bare has been a gift. What was taken from me was not my *self,* not the essential core of my being, but an identity I and others had created, the various personas necessary for functioning within social relationships. My mistake was in confusing these masks with my true self, so that when these were torn away, it seemed nothing was left. I was wrong. *I* was left, and with little to obstruct the view or distract the attention, I can see that the *I* is beloved of God.

As the turmoil of the past year subsides, I feel, paradoxical to say, an unsettling calm—unsettling, I suppose, because it disturbs the disturbance, and over time, even suffering can provide a comfortable familiarity. But I'm happy for it, this new disturbance, this *un*disturbance, for it is something like what I imagine William feels as he rides effortlessly on the shoulders of an unseen power.

Here at the beach, it's nice to be barefoot. Now, more than ever, I want to kick off my shoes, for the sand feels like holy ground. In this place on the margins I have become increasingly aware of One standing near me, the Marginal Man, One whose eternal place was in between: he hung on a cross stretched between earth and heaven, the mediator between our humanity and the Mystery of God.

After he died his followers returned to the sea and their boats. Perhaps they were simply returning to the familiar; perhaps they didn't know what else to do. But I believe, after this year, that some deep instinct drew them to the Deep, that their dark disappointment needed to be near the water. And it is not surprising that Jesus, after his resurrection, appeared to them there. After a fish fry on the beach, he said to Peter, the disciple who had failed so spectacularly, "Follow me."

If I have been drawn to the water's edge, it may be that I have been called here, by name. And if I have heard the wisdom of pelicans, it may have its origins in the One through whom all things, even pelicans, have been created. And if this is true, then this, too, is more than a possibility: even as the tragedy of the cross was turned, by God's grace, into the world's redemption, my own tawdry failures can be transformed into something useful and good and maybe even holy.

The details of my future remain hidden. What position I will have, where we will live, how I will earn income—these things are as clear to me as the ocean floor. But my calling is plain. I have been kept alive by a God who has opened her chest and bared her heart and fed me with her own life; I have been nourished back from starvation by self-sacrificing love. What else can I do but try to pattern my life on this self-giving? This is my inescapable vocation, it seems to me. I am asked to love as I have been loved.

There is no happiness in its opposite, as I can attest from too long a season of self-absorption. However necessary this sojourn into darkness, it must come to an end. The loss I have not wanted must be filled by a loss I happily assume. It's time to give myself, to offer my own blood to feed some starving chicks. My scarlet letter must be transformed into a scarlet badge of sacrifice.

When Dr. Albert Schweitzer visited the United States, he was asked by a reporter, "Have you found happiness in Africa?" He replied, "I have found a place of service, and that is enough happiness for anyone."[4]

I hope there might eventually be seen, at the tip of my bill, a permanent stain.

About a year ago my wife and I were given a splendid gift from dear friends—the use of a condominium on the sands of Cozumel, Mexico. We had just been through the horrific days of the Church's official condemnation and rejection, and our spirits were bruised and bloodied. We enjoyed the relaxation as the warm waters of the Caribbean soothed our wounds. But we could not escape the realities of our situation.

One morning before dawn I walked out onto a narrow spit of rock jutting into the water, and I sat down to wait. Wait for what? I couldn't have said, exactly, except it seemed the right thing to do. The arriving light revealed only gray—sea and sky were blended into one hard, impenetrable wall. My fear spoke out a prayer, or maybe it was an accusation: "God, that's exactly what the future is for me. A dull blankness. I see nothing at all."

Then I remembered the day before. I had been snorkeling. This was not my first time, but that day something happened between me and the water I will never forget. I was transfixed, mesmerized by beauty: brilliantly arrayed fish—blue angels and yellow tigers and orange clowns—and stingrays floating along the sand and coral rising like jagged mountain ranges around me. I had descended into another realm, a realm far from investigating committees and aggressive reporters, a blessed realm of beauty and peace. This is what I recalled as I sat on that spit of rock. The sea was not empty. Just beneath the surface it was an explosion of color and an abundance of life, and once again my heart seemed to beat with the pulse of creation, and I experienced the joy, the childlike delight of being in the midst of it all. And I laughed aloud—laughed at my blind stupidity. "Forgive me," I said. "I see so little, so very little."

NOTES

Chapter 1: At the Margins

1. Rachel Carson, *The Edge of the Sea* (Boston: Houghton Mifflin, 1955), p. 1.

2. Lena Lencek and Gideon Bosker, *The Beach: A History of Paradise on Earth* (New York: Penguin, 1998), p. xxiv.

3. E. B. White, "The Sea and the Wind That Blows," *Essays of E. B. White* (New York: Harper Colophon Books, 1977), p. 206.

4. Anne Morrow Lindbergh, *Gift from the Sea* (New York: Vintage Books, 1955), pp. 16–17.

5. Dan Guravich and Joseph E. Brown, *The Return of the Brown Pelican* (Baton Rouge: Louisiana State University, 1983), p. 2.

6. Ibid., p. 23.

Chapter 2: William's Bill

1. I deal with this theme more fully in *Waking from the American Dream: Growing Through Your Disappointments* (Downers Grove, Ill.: InterVarsity Press, 1988).

2. Parker J. Palmer, *Let Your Life Speak: Listening for the Voice of Vocation* (San Francisco: Jossey-Bass, 2000), p. 39.

3. Augustine, *Confessions,* Pine-Coffin, trans. (London: Penguin Books, 1985), p. 169.

4. Ralph Ellison, "Richard Wright's Blues," *The Collected Essays of Ralph Ellison* (New York: The Modern Library, 1995), p. 129.

5. Nathaniel Hawthorne, *The Scarlet Letter* (New York: Penguin Classics, 1986), p. 50.

6. Ibid.

7. Thomas Moore, *The Soul of Sex: Cultivating Life as an Act of Love* (New York: HarperCollins, 1998), p. 75.

Chapter 3: Diving Deep

1. Dan Guravich and Joseph E. Brown, *The Return of the Brown Pelican* (Baton Rouge: Louisiana State University, 1983), p. 83.
2. Annie Dillard, *The Writing Life* (New York: Harper and Row, 1989), pp. 78–79.
3. As quoted by John R. W. Stott, "The Up-to-the-Minute Relevance of the Resurrection," *Preaching Today,* tape number 79.
4. Ernest Becker, *The Denial of Death* (New York: Free Press Paperbacks Edition, 1997), p. 11.
5. Ibid., pp. 18, 23, 145–46.
6. Alfred, Lord Tennyson, *In Memoriam A. H. H.,* in *In Memoriam,* ed. Robert H. Ross (New York: W. W. Norton, 1973), p. 62.
7. Alan Jones, *The Soul's Journey* (San Francisco: HarperSanFrancisco, 1995), p. 47.

Chapter 4: Taking Off

1. Rollo May, *Love and Will* (New York: Norton, 1969), pp. 74–75.
2. Ephesians 5:31–32 (New Revised Standard Version).
3. Frederick Buechner, *The Hungering Dark* (New York: Seabury, 1969), p. 83.
4. Ibid.

Chapter 5: Rituals of Preparation

1. Dan Guravich and Joseph E. Brown, *The Return of the Brown Pelican* (Baton Rouge: Louisiana State University Press, 1983), p. 72.
2. Rollo May, *The Courage to Create* (New York: Bantam, 1975), pp. 65–67.
3. As quoted by Fred B. Craddock, *As One Without Authority* (Nashville: Abingdon, 1979), p. 101.
4. Dan Wakefield, *Returning: A Spiritual Journey* (New York: Doubleday, 1988), p. 178.

Chapter 6: Letting Go

1. Andrew Sullivan, "Calling Off the Hounds," *Time,* January 29, 2001, n.p.

2. Saul Bellow, *Herzog* (New York: Penguin Books, 1996), p. 169.

3. Ecclesiastes 3:5–6 (New Revised Standard Version).

Chapter 7: Guano on the Head

1. Dan Guravich and Joseph E. Brown, *The Return of the Brown Pelican* (Baton Rouge: Louisiana State University Press, 1983), p. 24.

2. William White, "Stories for Telling," *Parables, Etc.,* February 1990, p. 9.12.2.

3. Philippians 4:8 (New Revised Standard Version).

4. Luke 23:34 (New Revised Standard Version).

5. As quoted in Rick Lance, "Following in His Footsteps," *Preaching,* July–August 1989, p. 20.

Chapter 8: Flying Together

1. *The Constitution of the Presbyterian Church (U.S.A.), Part II, Book of Order 1999–2000,* D-1.0102.

2. Ernest Becker, *The Denial of Death* (New York: Free Press Paperbacks Edition, 1977), p. 136.

3. Galatians 6:2 (New Revised Standard Version).

4. John 3:17 (New Revised Standard Version).

Chapter 9: Held Aloft

1. I John 4:16 (New Revised Standard Version).

2. Paul Tillich, *The Shaking of the Foundations* (New York: Charles Scribner's Sons, 1948), p. 162.

3. Romans 7:20 (New Revised Standard Version).

4. As quoted by Clifford Williams, "When Mercy Hurts," *Christianity Today,* February 3, 1989, p. 16.

5. Gerard Manley Hopkins, "The Windhover," *The Major Poems* (London: J. M. Dent, 1979), p. 67.

Chapter 10: Silence

1. Dan Guravich and Joseph E. Brown, *The Return of the Brown Pelican* (Baton Rouge: Louisiana State University Press, 1983), p. 47.

2. As quoted in Eugene Peterson, *Reversed Thunder* (San Francisco: Harper and Row, 1988), p. 192.

3. As quoted in "To Quote . . . ," *Leadership,* Spring 1997, p. 73.

4. *The American Heritage Dictionary of the English Language,* Third Edition (Boston: Houghton Mifflin, 1996), p. 1721.

5. Clifton Fadiman, ed., *The Little, Brown Book of Anecdotes* (Boston: Little, Brown, 1985), p. 195.

6. T. S. Eliot, "Ash Wednesday," *Collected Poems: 1909–1962* (New York: Harcourt Brace, 1963), p. 86.

7. Richard Wightman Fox, *Trials of Intimacy: Love and Loss in the Beecher-Tilton Scandal* (Chicago: University of Chicago Press, 1999), p. 44.

8. Isaiah 30:15 (New Revised Standard Version).

Chapter 11: Forces Beyond Control

1. In the preceding discussion of the decline and return of brown pelicans, I am deeply indebted to Dan Guravich and Joseph E. Brown, *The Return of the Brown Pelican* (Baton Rouge: Louisiana State University Press, 1983).

2. As quoted in Eugene Peterson, *Answering God: The Psalms as Tools for Prayer* (San Francisco: HarperSanFrancisco, 1989), p. 45.

Chapter 12: Back to Origins

1. Roger Rosenblatt, "I Am Writing Blindly," *Time,* November 6, 2000, p. 142.

2. See Christoph Gerhardt, *Die Metamorphosen des Pelikans* (Frankfurt am Main: Peter Lang, 1979).

3. Will D. Campbell, *Brother to a Dragonfly* (New York: Seabury, 1977), p. 18.

4. *Parables, Etc.,* volume 9, number 9, November 1989, p. 5.